Going for Growth

Going for Growth

How to grow your business on a budget

Emma Jones

Published in association with

HARRIMAN HOUSE LTD
18 College Street
Petersfield
Hampshire
GU31 4AD
GREAT BRITAIN
Tel: +44 (0)1730 233870

Email: enquiries@harriman-house.com
Website: www.harriman-house.com

First published in Great Britain in 2015.

Paperback ISBN: 978-0-85719-472-5
eBook ISBN: 978-0-85719-473-2

British Library Cataloguing in Publication Data
A CIP catalogue record for this book can be obtained from the British Library.

Cover arrows by Iveta Angelova/Shutterstock.
Chapter icons by ©iStockphoto.com/sodafish, ©iStockphoto.com/lushik and colorsark/Creative Market.

This book is dedicated to the Enterprise Nation team and community.
Together we are building a true Enterprise Nation.

Contents

Introduction

Over the past couple of years I have watched with interest as businesses profiled in our books and on the blog, event attendees, and Enterprise Nation members have grown in a most modern way.

It's a form of growth we have adopted at Enterprise Nation.

And it's a route to growth I've been repeating at every available opportunity to government.

I thought it was time to write it down.

The result is a book that shows how business owners are growing profitable and successful businesses without taking on high risk and high costs.

It suggests the way in which businesses are growing has changed and government policies and programmes must adapt to reward and recognise businesses for increasing profits over headcount, and creating wealth as opposed to employment.

To compile the book, I returned to businesses I've profiled over the past six years – from my first book *Spare Room Start Up* to subsequent titles *Working 5 to 9* and *Go Global* – to ask them how they have grown. Added to their stories are 27 more.

There is one common factor amongst all the case studies: They are small businesses with big ambitions.

The owners and founders want to succeed but not at the price of giving up the role in the business they most enjoy. They are focusing on what they do best and outsourcing the rest; they are proving their business model before franchising it to others, and boxing up knowledge and selling it via digital platforms. They are creating networked companies, going global, and being accelerated by major brands.

Most of the businesses started at home but, naturally, a few have taken the decision to move out. After nine years of building her business Labels4Kids, Ann-Maree Morrison has bought a property so her three sons can claim back their house from employees working in the kitchen, spare room and hall! And Adrianna Cadwallader of Saturday Sewing Session moved her studio out of home to create a space for her own designs, as well as to tutor others.

What unites all the businesses profiled in this book – and many more like them – is that they are growing a business whilst staying nimble, and scaling whilst keeping true to their entrepreneurial roots.

By embracing technology and reaching out for advice, they are running (in some cases) multi-million pound businesses and educating the next generation of entrepreneurs as a good number of them remain home-based.

This is the story of how they have achieved it – how you can too – and what the government should do to support even more of it.

Emma Jones

About the Author

Emma Jones is founder of Enterprise Nation (www.enterprisenation.com) and author of bestselling books including *Spare Room Start Up*, *Working 5 to 9* and *Go Global*.

Following a degree in Law and Japanese, Emma joined international accounting firm Arthur Andersen, where she worked in the London, Leeds and Manchester offices and set up the firm's Inward Investment practice that attracted overseas companies to locate in the UK. Bitten by the dot com bug, Emma left the firm in 2000 to start her first business, Techlocate – and after 15 months the company was successfully sold to Tenon plc.

The experience of starting, growing and selling a business from home gave Emma the idea for Enterprise Nation, which was launched in 2006 as a home business website. The company has expanded to become the UK's most active small business network, with over 65,000 businesses receiving support via accessing content, advice, events and funding, and having their views represented to government.

In 2011 Emma was one of eight co-founders of StartUp Britain; a national enterprise campaign which she led for three years. Over that time the campaign hosted Industry Weeks, toured the UK with entrepreneurs and experts, launched special projects such as PopUp Britain and played a critical role in record results of people becoming their own boss.

Emma was awarded an MBE for services to enterprise in July 2012.

Profiled Case Studies

Alex Gooch, Artisan Baker	www.alexgoochbaker.com
Alison Battisby	www.alisonbattisby.com
Blonde & Ginger	www.blondeandginger.com
BoginaBag	www.boginabag.com
Coco Rose London	www.cocoroselondon.com
Digital Dragonfly	www.digitaldragonfly.co.uk
iPilates	www.ipilates.co.uk
Jamsmith	www.jamsmith.co.uk
Jonny's Sister	www.jonnyssister.co.uk
Labels4Kids	www.labels4kids.com
Loafkins	www.loafkins.com
Mr Singh's	www.mrsinghssauce.co.uk
My Secret Kitchen	www.mysecretkitchen.co.uk
PaperBoy Interiors	www.paperboywallpaper.co.uk
Petshopbowl	www.petshopbowl.co.uk
Pinucci	www.pinucci.com
Pyjama Drama	www.pyjamadrama.com

Rapanui Clothing	www.rapanuiclothing.com
Raring2Go	www.raring2go.co.uk
Riverford	www.riverford.co.uk
Rock n Roll Bride	www.rocknrollbride.com
Sarah J Thomas photography	www.sarahjthomas.com
Saturday Sewing Session	www.saturdaysewingsession.co.uk
Shedworking	www.shedworking.co.uk
Shoo Rayner	www.shoorayner.com
smallcarBIGCITY	www.smallcarbigcity.com
Snact	www.snact.co.uk
Time etc	www.timeetc.com
The PR Network	www.theprnetwork.co.uk
The Travelwrap Company	www.thetravelwrapcompany.com
Trinkets	www.trinketwomen.com
Turbine	www.turbinehq.com
Tutor2u	www.tutor2u.net
Twisted Twee	www.twistedtwee.co.uk
Women Unlimited	www.womenunlimited.com

Part I. Making the Case for Modern Growth

Growth but not as we know it

An increasing number of businesses in Britain are growing by outsourcing and subcontracting to experts, as opposed to recruiting full-time staff. They are creating franchise organisations and offering an opportunity for thousands more to go self-employed. They are selling their knowledge by harnessing technology and powerful channels to market, with help from professionals who aren't on the payroll. It's a sensible and low-risk way to grow and enables the business owner to:

Recruit the best

Top talent is readily available as record numbers of people turn to self-employment to do the work they enjoy. Looking for a lawyer to advise on intellectual property protection for a new product? That would be former top corporate lawyer and now founder of a specialist small business legal outfit, Joanna Tall. Want branding advice from the person who founded one of the most famous ad agencies in the land? Your man is Andy Law. These are just two examples of the top talent now available and working with small businesses on an outsourced and self-employed basis, as opposed to full-time and in-house.

UK businesses have posted over 344,000 jobs on global talent marketplace oDesk, making the UK one of the most active markets on the platform and highlighting the fact that small business owners are finding the talent and personnel they need via online marketplaces and business networks. A listing of these talent marketplaces can be found in the table 'Top 10 sites on which to find the talent you're after' on page 168.

Disregard geography

Small businesses are spreading wealth across the nation by employing designers from Devon, accountants in Anglesey and Mancunian PR pros! The point is, with management tools such as Skype and Basecamp (which are covered in the Technology section) there's no need to work in the same location. Small business owners are more likely to hire for skill and sector expertise, as opposed to geographic proximity.

Compare this with a business being run from a traditional office. It is more likely to require staff to work from a single site and so restrict its radius for attracting talent.

Manage overheads

Bringing on extra resource when it's needed – and scaling back when it's not – is an advisable way to grow. In the words of one entrepreneur: "Your objective as a business owner is to keep costs as low as possible, for as long as possible". This is how Barnaby

Lashbrooke decided to grow his Virtual PA business, Time etc, profiled on page 10.

Outsourcing is a way to test performance without having to commit to long-term contracts. A few months of working with an outsourced partner or freelance contractor will help you determine if you want to keep that contract renewed.

Build a brand

When your workforce is made up of freelancers and fellow business owners, you don't have to spend so much time managing people. Your team is already motivated to deliver a good service, with their own business reputation depending on it.

Time saved on managing and motivating can be directed at building your company ethos and vision. People may be working for you as self-employed individuals but a sense of loyalty can be created towards the brand and your objectives. This is something that's covered in the Talent Manager section.

> *"Whether I see the Enterprise Nation team face to face or not, I still feel fully engaged as I share their unboundless energy for work and life, which threads through everything we strive to achieve in the business – and this motivates me every single day."*
>
> Lorna Bladen, Head of events, Enterprise Nation

Name: Barnaby Lashbrooke

Business: Time etc

The experience of starting and selling a first business gave Barnaby Lashbrooke the idea for his second.

"I wondered why there wasn't a way to get the help I needed running the business, without hiring and going to expensive agencies."

Spotting a gap in the market led to the launch of Time etc in 2007. The company gives small businesses access to talented people, by the hour.

"You can get your business tasks, from admin to marketing, done by carefully hand-picked and talented people in the UK and only pay for the work they do. It's a way for small businesses to get access to brilliant people who have worked for organisations like Apple, the BBC and AOL at a fraction of the cost of employing them directly."

The company has over 200 Time etc agents and is growing constantly. The agents are self-employed and from all over the UK and USA.

"Between 2007 and 2012 we didn't use freelancers to do tasks for our clients – we recruited full-time assistants in Birmingham city centre. Keeping hold of young ambitious people was a real struggle, as was finding enough people with the skills our clients needed at a price they could afford. We took a risk – changed the business model – and have since experienced much higher growth. Our original team of full-time employees has slowly, naturally reduced as we have grown through a vibrant network of self-motivated and self-employed agents."

The company is seeing an increase in the number of small businesses wanting to outsource tasks to Time etc.

"In both the UK and USA we're seeing that outsourcing is becoming commonplace and well understood. The difference between now and when we started in 2007 is remarkable."

Barnaby is also seeing a growth in the number of people wanting to become Time etc agents. The company is selective in the agents it chooses, spending time sourcing the best talent available.

"There are some remarkable people out there who are delighted to find flexible work that they can do from home when it suits them."

With 200 agents, Time etc uses technology developed in-house to help freelancers manage their workload and communicate with clients.

"We make heavy use of Skype and have a central team who do regular outreach to our freelancers to make sure they have everything they need. We're quite respectful of the fact that our freelancers are self-employed and we try to act more like a partner than an employer."

The company has ambitious growth plans of its own.

"The next 12 months should be big for us. We're about 10% of the way into a dramatic growth plan that includes opening lots of new routes to market and automating the delivery of the service. We're tripling our marketing budget for the coming year which is very exciting – the first time we've had a marketing plan of that scale."

 www.timeetc.com

 @timeetc

In survey after survey, Enterprise Nation members tell us they're planning to grow, but not via the traditional route of hiring people and acquiring offices.

Results from January 2015 show 80% of respondents optimistic of business growth with only 16% saying this will come from taking on employees. Growth is being delivered by entering new markets, acquiring bigger customers and launching new products and services. The manpower required to fuel this is being met by a creative network of entrepreneurial individuals.

The rise of the micro-enterprise

What we are witnessing is the rise of the modern micro-enterprise; an enterprise that increases turnover whilst staying nimble, and embraces technology to rapidly move into new markets.

Many of the entrepreneurs driving these operations are choosing to not only start, but also to grow the business from home as the infrastructure is in place to outsource everything from fulfilment to finance. Space and people may still be a requirement to grow but you don't have to own these assets outright.

Staying home-based means spending time and money in the local economy and educating the next generation of entrepreneurs. Niamh Barker has six young entrepreneurs on her team as she runs the highly successful Travelwrap Company from a converted garage and around the family.

Name: Niamh Barker

Company: The Travelwrap Company

Before launching The Travelwrap Company Niamh Barker was a pharmacist by profession, having worked in hospitals, and in the pharmaceutical industry for ten years.

"After getting married I had two children (and acquired four stepchildren!) and wanted to do something that would fit alongside family life but provide a vehicle for my creative inclination. I also wanted to do something commercially successful that was more than a 'kitchen table' business."

The Travelwrap Company was founded in August 2007 and the signature product, the Scottish cashmere Travelwrap, went on to win Luxury Gift of the Year in 2013. The inspiration for the product came from Niamh's own business travel.

"I hated the idea of the reusable acrylic blanket on planes and my idea was to allow travellers to have a beautiful knitted cashmere travel blanket that would provide comfort and a sense of home. I also felt I had the personal determination and commercial experience to create an original luxury British brand that would be successful in the UK and internationally."

Niamh's vision is being realised and The Travelwrap Company is fast becoming an internationally-recognised luxury British brand with online sales to eight countries and wholesale to 15 countries.

"We have had enormous support from UK Trade & Investment (UKTI) who have provided expert trade advice and practical support for our business. All sorts of services are offered and often subsidised or match-funded. We had a 'Communications Review' of our website which helped with the basic milestones of building parallel international websites (which are relevant and can be seen by the country you are targeting) to, for example, finding an expert for me to talk through import duties in Canada. Alongside the expertise and advice, we've also attended trade missions and Embassy showcases where we can explore the market and make contact with relevant buyers. Trade shows overseas are expensive and a risk if you don't know the market. These showcases allow us to 'dip our toe' and make sure the audience is a good fit for us."

As well as making sales overseas, Niamh is stepping up activity to make corporate sales. Her signature Travelwrap lends itself well to corporate and guest gifting.

"Corporate gifting is a difficult market to target as it really is all about networking and finding appropriate clients. So far we have collaborated with cruise ship companies, high-end automobile companies and are currently working on a great collaboration with the St. Regis Hotel Group."

Niamh realised early on that she would not be able to afford the conventional marketing routes for promoting her luxury brand.

"We would have needed to advertise in broadsheets and expensive glossies to make that work and it was – and still is – cost-prohibitive for us, so instead I started building relationships with journalists in the travel, business and fashion press. We have a unique and gorgeous product and I'm passionate about the business so I manage to achieve quite a lot of column inches just on the back of that! For example, I remember reading a piece by *The Telegraph* business editor one Sunday afternoon and then tracking down his email address to tell him the story of the Travelwrap Company for the section's start-up column. It took quite a lot of persistence and time but a few months later we had a half-page interview in *The Telegraph* – that worked very well for business."

This ambitious and growing business started life in the spare room, which meant having to move everything to one side when visitors showed up!

"We had a fairly big garage space which we converted into two small offices. Inevitably business and home flow into each other but at least now I can close the door on the office at the end of the day. I do love the fact that I waste none of my day commuting and can start my working day at a ridiculous time of the morning (about 5am usually) so that I can come back into the house for breakfast at 7.30 ...having done 2.5 hours work before the rest of the household gets up!

Without my little dream team of a family I would have had no chance of getting the business to where it is today. My husband is part of the management team (alongside working full-time himself) and a wizard on spreadsheets, which is great as I am most definitely not! My dear parents-in-law have packed so many travelwraps over the years that they could easily get a job in a cashmere mill! My children and step children put up with mummy juggling conference calls and dinner very regularly, and recently my 10-year-old crawled across my office to reach something she wanted in my handbag while I was on a Skype call to China.

When I am due to go away it is a bit of a military operation getting me on the plane and ensuring everyone has what they will need while I'm travelling, but with the help of FaceTime and Ocado deliveries we all survive and, actually, I think it is a great message for children these days...for them to see a little business develop and grow and the joys and tears along the way!"

In terms of employing people outside the family, Niamh needs to gear things up between September and the end of January which is when around 60% of company sales happen.

"My pool of talent often comes from the big population of very capable and well-qualified women that don't work on a daily basis but are enthusiastic, energetic and trustworthy."

With a supportive family and energetic supporters around her, Niamh is all set for the next 12 months.

"It will be more of the same of the last 12 really. Our sales have grown over 60% in the last year and we're looking to repeat that. Our biggest growth revenue is export and that is what will continue to attract our attention, without losing sight of our valuable UK market of course. We have already explored a couple of new markets this year including UAE and China, both of which we still need to do a lot of work on. There are a couple of other markets I would like to visit in the next 12 months to explore and network, including the USA and Australia, but neither do I think we can conquer the world in a year!"

 **www.thetravelwrapcompany.com**

 **@travelwrap**

Multiply this contribution to the economy, and positive impact on society, by the three-million-plus micro-businesses of Britain and what you get is a powerful force.

It is the proposition of this book that the form of growth we are seeing, powered by small businesses across the country and across all sectors, should be noted, understood, recognised and celebrated by the institutions speaking on behalf of our nation.

Out of touch

Some large institutions are yet to catch up with what's happening on the ground when it comes to small business. They hold two distinct misconceptions:

People turn to self-employment because they can't find a job

Following the release of figures from the Office for National Statistics in April 2014 showing surging self-employment, outdated organisations presented this as a sign of a weak labour market. 'People are starting businesses because they can't find jobs,' suggested the TUC on BBC's *Newsnight*.

How wrong. And how rooted in an industrial past.

The second misconception is this:

Once started, the main aim of a business is to create jobs

"Britain's surge in self-employment is being driven by people working for themselves, rather than starting job-creating businesses, according to research that will spark fresh debate about the country's entrepreneurial drive," headlined Brian Groom in the *Financial Times* on 14th April 2014.

Media channels have yet to extensively report on the millions of self-employed who are actively creating 'wealth' as opposed to 'jobs'.

The Bank of England is getting close to recognising self-employment as a structural change in the economy with the Monetary Policy Committee stating:

> "Part of the rise in self-employment appeared to be a continuation of a longer term secular trend, rather than a cyclical response to a lack of other employment opportunities."

But the ultimate body to influence is government, as the institution creates policy which can help or hinder growth.

Modern growth

The Chancellor is a keen champion of growth. It is a word he uses regularly – and it is almost always followed by the word 'employment'. This is a chancellor who believes growth comes from employment and the way to grow is to encourage businesses to hire and create jobs.

> "This is a government whose plan is delivering jobs."
>
> – George Osborne, Budget, March 2014
>
> "Today I'm making a new commitment – a commitment to fight for full employment in Britain. I want to make the UK the best place in the world to create a job; to get a job; to keep a job; to be helped to look for another job if you lose one."
>
> – George Osborne, 1 April 2014

The Chancellor's vision is backed by a long-term economic plan of five points, of which point three is:

> 'Creating more jobs. By backing small business and enterprise with better infrastructure and lower jobs taxes.'

This is translated into action through the introduction of programmes for small business that are focused on – you guessed it – creating jobs!

In September 2010, the National Insurance Contributions (NICs) holiday for new businesses came into effect.

> "New business set up outside London, the South East and East of England will be eligible for a holiday worth up to £5,000 for up to the first ten employees they hire in their first year of business. The scheme will run for three years. It is estimated that 400,000 new businesses will benefit by having a lower tax bill from employing new staff."
>
> – Gov.uk (www.gov.uk/government/news/national-insurance-holiday-for-new-businesses-in-the-regions-begins)

In August 2013, and following a Freedom of Information Request, Asa Bennett of *The Huffington Post* reported that 24,000 businesses had applied for the NICs holiday, meaning:

> "The scheme has achieved 6% of its target near the end of its planned duration."
>
> – www.huffingtonpost.co.uk/2013/08/10/national-insurance-holiday-flop_n_3737200.html

Despite the low take-up, the decision was made to go further. The Chancellor announced a new Employment Allowance to replace the NIC holiday and expanded it to employers across the UK, offering a reduction on NICs for employees by up to £2,000. "Up to 1.25 million businesses and charities will benefit," claimed the government.

This scheme appears to be faring better. As of January 2015, six months after introduction, 856,000 employers had claimed the Allowance.

But as former Enterprise Nation editor, Simon Wicks states:

> "Policies to make it easier to take on employees, including National Insurance holidays, though welcome, will only ever touch a minority of businesses.
>
> Policies aimed at making workplaces easier to rent or buy, or tax breaks based on traditional premises, though welcome, will only ever touch a minority of businesses."

Is it time to review the programmes that reward businesses for growth; to include incentives for hiring as well as incentives for growing in a modern and flexible way of increasing turnover, not headcount?

Let's change the vision to:

> 'Creating more ~~jobs~~ enterprise. By backing small business and enterprise with better infrastructure and lower ~~jobs~~ sales taxes.'

There are a number of existing and helpful programmes relevant to businesses growing in this modern way. At Enterprise Nation, we'd like to see them extended and increased!

- **Shares for freelancers** – keen to encourage employee ownership, the government is introducing models and backing businesses that adopt the John Lewis approach where employees become partners and benefit from the company's success. We would like to see this model of employee ownership made available to business owners wanting to reward shares to freelancers and contractors.
- **Access to new markets** – with businesses stating growth comes from entering new markets and selling to larger customers, there is a role for government to highlight its target of buying 25% of all its products and services from small businesses by May 2015 and, critically, training and education on how to go about tendering. To encourage contracts between big and

small, the Corporate Venturing Scheme could be reinstated and extended to offer incentives for large corporates to buy from small business, as well as invest in them.

- **Access to advice** – the government's Growth Vouchers programme, introduced in January 2014, has successfully started to change the culture whereby business owners now see the value of accessing professional advice to grow. This programme, considered a success by participating advisers and Growth Voucher recipients, is due to cease in March 2015. For the sake of modern British business growth, Enterprise Nation is pushing for its continuation, with funds directed from the private sector so there is no cost to the public purse.
- **Space for growth** – businesses need places to meet partners and collaborate with peers. The government is opening up its own space to small business through a Space for Growth programme. This is a good intention but there are currently very few options promoted via this initiative and there's potential for more space to open up from libraries, post offices and closed-down bank branches. These unused spaces could be put to good use by small businesses for co-working and/or PopUp shops.
- **Simplify tax** – one of the reasons small business owners shy away from hiring is on account of the admin that comes with it. Simplify tax and its processes by creating a new sales tax to replace business income tax, Class 4 National Insurance, corporation tax and VAT. Enterprise Nation is actively campaigning for such a move and will continue to do so.

There is a role for big business too in securing productive growth.

- **Procurement** – open up your supply chains and buy the new products and fresh talent on offer from small businesses. As above, this could be enhanced by pushing for reintroduction of the Corporate Venturing Scheme.
- **Accelerate** – brands including Cisco, John Lewis, Tesco and Telefonica are launching labs, competitions and accelerators to give small businesses access to market and surrounding them with infrastructure. (These are covered in 'Move In' on page 198.) We want to see more corporate-backed projects that offer this in-built support.
- **Prompt payment** – according to Enterprise Nation research, the majority of businesses surveyed say they are not looking to take on debt, loans or equity to grow. But they do need to be paid on time. Prompt payment creates a satisfied network of suppliers and avoids damaging cash flow issues.

With government and big business creating the conditions for growth, attention now turns to you, the business owner, and how you can make the most of these conditions.

Part II. Grow the Business on a Budget

Know your niche

These are three words I repeat often when advising small businesses. It applies here as a first and fundamental step before growing the business. Knowing your niche involves knowing:

- what distinct product or service you're offering
- which clearly identifiable group you're offering it to.

The benefits of a niche business are keeping your marketing costs low as you know where your customers are, what they're buying, and their key influencers, and keeping loyalty high as customers can only buy what they're after from you. Knowing your niche is the springboard from which you can expand.

Here are two business owners profiled in this book highlighting the benefits:

"I've always been an advocate for specialising in a certain area of photography rather than spreading your time too thinly between genres such as children, portraits, weddings, etc. It's always been my opinion that being a specialist in your field is essential and that the skills required for wedding photography (for example) are very different to those of a child photographer. Yes, technically it doesn't matter but the people skills, marketing and branding are very different beasts. I do however see the value in diversifying your business and developing your specialist brand."

Sarah J Thomas, specialist in child photography

"Focusing on a niche and having a very clear and simple message has allowed us to get our message across easily and effectively. It's quite clear what we do from the name of the brand and also from the 'About' page on the website. There is no confusion as to who we are/what we do/what we make so I think this has made us quite a memorable brand for both the media and our customers. In terms of press coverage it helps too. Doing a piece on decorating for boys? Who are you going to get in touch with ... PaperBoy (well, hopefully!)."

Victoria Cramsie, Founder of Paperboy Wallpaper

In both these businesses, the owners clearly know what they are offering to whom and this helps deepen expertise, relations with customers, and links with the media. Know your niche and these next steps will be much more straightforward.

Franchise

Grow your business by developing a trading record and creating a franchise package for entrepreneurial individuals who help you rapidly expand the business and the brand

Growing through franchise is particularly suited to companies that have a model which is easily transferable and has a process to follow for making a profit. For example, dance activities for children or tasting parties for food fans. The aim is to perfect a model that works in one area and then grow by enabling others to replicate it. According to the British Franchise Association, the official description of franchising is:

> "The granting of a licence by one person (the franchisor) to another (the franchisee), which entitles the franchisee to trade as their own business under the brand of the franchisor, following a proven business model. The franchisee also receives a package, comprising all the elements necessary to establish a previously untrained person in the business and to run it with continual assistance on a predetermined basis (including a predetermined agreement length – with renewal options)."

It is an increasingly popular way for business owners to grow as it is achievable at a low cost and at high speed:

- **Low cost** – as the capital required for expansion comes from the franchisees who pay a fee to buy the model and apply it in their area
- **High speed** – as you license the business to entrepreneurial individuals who are motivated to grow and, often, based in the territory of expansion

Taking this route to growth does, though, require an investment of time in perfecting the business model and money to develop the franchise package.

Perfecting the model

Some years ago I interviewed Sinclair Beecham, one of the two founders of Pret A Manger. He explained how he and his partner spent seven years in their first shop in Victoria perfecting every aspect of the business from the taste of the sandwich to the training of staff. Only then did they feel able to replicate the model in shop number two. Now there are 295 Pret shops across the globe generating an annual turnover of £380 million. You could say those first seven years were time well spent in getting the model just right so it was ripe for expansion.

Drama teacher Sarah Owen spent three years perfecting the model for her Pyjama Drama activity classes for kids.

Name: Sarah Owen

Business: Pyjama Drama

As a drama teacher, Sarah Owen could see the benefits young children derived from drama and music classes; in the form of fun but also in increasing their confidence. Sarah launched Pyjama Drama in 2005 to deliver such classes in her own town of Powys, North Wales.

"I ran Pyjama Drama classes for three years before taking the decision to franchise in 2008. During that time I refined and perfected the classes and developed all the original songs and music that we have. When looking at the options for expansion, franchising seemed the most logical route."

After a few false starts, Sarah found a good lawyer and franchise consultant based on recommendations from others who were established in franchising. The company now has 29 franchises across the UK with more in the pipeline. Sarah and her business partner, Katie Moffat, receive a constant stream of enquiries from overseas but have taken the decision to remain focused on the UK for now. In Sarah's mind, the greatest challenge comes with balancing time between working on the business and managing franchisees.

"When you're starting off you imagine that you will reach a time where all the systems and processes are in place and it will simply be a case of managing and supporting the franchisees but you never stop wanting to improve and develop the business. In the end it comes down to being very organised about how you manage your time and it's also important to have a great team behind you."

With franchisees requiring support to help them start and grow, Sarah has put full-time resources in place, believing the more you help and nurture your franchisees, the more their businesses will develop – growing your business in the process.

When it comes to Sarah's one top tip for business owners considering franchising, she says:

"Spend time finding a recommended franchise consultant and good legal advice. You can try and work it all out yourself but there is a tremendous amount you have to be aware of if you want a robust business."

In Sarah's case, she turned for advice to seasoned franchise entrepreneur Lee Dancy, the entrepreneur behind Home from Home Pet Care franchise Barking Mad, which has over 60 franchises in the UK and is growing rapidly overseas. Lee sits as a non-executive director of Pyjama Drama, lending her experience and expertise. "Lee's input has been invaluable," says Sarah, "as she has been through this journey herself, it provides a shortcut for us so we save time but also know we're setting things up right and in the interests of our franchises who, after all, are the beating heart of the business."

 **www.pyjamadrama.com**

 **@pyjama_drama**

The business model Sarah and Katie had created was one that appealed to Lisa Armstrong; a working mum from Glasgow who was looking for a business opportunity to run around her family. Lisa became a Pyjama Drama franchisee in December 2011 and started trading in April 2012.

View from a franchisee

"I was attracted to working with an established brand and saw it as an opportunity to bring the product to my area where I could see the potential. All the hard work had been done, e.g. product formulation, brand, website, systems, etc. and I would be free to focus on growing a business that excited me. I wanted the flexibility of being my own boss whilst getting support from other franchisees and head office.

To start, we had an intensive four-day training course at head office and then a two-day follow-up course three months later. Once training was completed, we had (and have) constant support and backup which is fantastic, including a field visit within three months to assess progress. We receive weekly updates and a weekly newsletter.

I have quarterly regional meetings with other franchisees to share ideas and provide a platform for feedback to head office. An annual conference and quarterly regional meetings allow for meeting up in person.

My plan is to grow the business by hiring a session leader to deliver more classes so I can spend more time raising our profile in Glasgow through social media and direct communication with existing and potential customers."

As well as franchising being a route that's increasingly popular amongst business owners, the same can be said for the number of franchisees, which stands at 40,000 people with many, like Lisa, wanting to be their own boss whilst adopting a proven business model and leveraging the support of a national team.

"The number of businesses using a franchise model to fuel their expansion has grown every year for over two decades, including right the way through the recession. It's a well-established and proven model to expand a business, but requires significant time and investment from the outset. Specialist advice from experienced sector professionals is essential to provide the platform for solid and consistent growth."

PAUL STAFFORD, BRITISH FRANCHISE ASSOCIATION

Perfecting the package

With the business model perfected, it's time to put together a franchise package that can be made available for sale. Work through this table of tasks so you are prepared when interested franchisees come to call.

Track record	*Ensure the business is a working model of success. Franchisees will pay money for something they can see has a clear path to profit. Be prepared to make your own accounts public or at least show what the franchisee can expect to earn if they follow the training and guidelines. The brand is also an asset that's being bought so ensure you rightfully own it with trademarks and intellectual property protection in place.*
Training	*The business model is something that has to be teachable i.e. you can train people (some of whom may be quite new to business) on how the operation works.*
Toolkit	*After training, provide a comprehensive toolkit or manual that guides the franchisee with tips on marketing, sales, finance and growing the business. The toolkit could also include marketing templates or collateral such as posters, stickers, flyers, etc.*
Technology	*Does the franchise involve a website for serving customers or intranet platform for accessing internal support? Either way, deliver an easy-to-use system with effective data collection so you can track progress and performance.*

Team	*Have you got the right team in place? A support resource for franchisees and support for you, the business owner, in the form of a mentor or adviser.*
Territory	*Is your franchise opportunity restricted to a certain territory i.e. a franchisee pays to have access to a particular geographic area? If so, define this from the start.*
Testimonials	*Consider doing deals in the early days so you can expand quite quickly. This will be a factor in future recruitment as potential franchisees will probably ask to speak with existing ones. Have some quotes available to offer.*
Termination	*Put provisions in place to terminate the agreement if it's not working – from either side!*

There are costs involved in developing the package with the main ones being:

- Professional fees for set-up
- Production of toolkit with marketing collateral
- Marketing and promoting the franchise
- Managing the franchise and providing support

"The franchisor investment is mainly at the outset prior to recruiting franchisees. The franchisees pay a franchise fee, which covers the costs of setting up the franchise: training, marketing, operations manuals, etc. The franchisor will start to see returns from the ongoing monthly management fees that the franchisee pays usually based on the business turnover figures. Recruiting the right franchisees is key to protecting the business brand and the ongoing franchise network."

CATHRYN A. HAYES, FRANCHISE UNIT, HSBC

There are a number of consultants, available for hire, to assist with turning your business into one that can be franchised. Paul Monaghan is director of one such consulting outfit – The Franchising Centre – and I asked him how much a business owner could be expected to pay for help with readying the business for franchise.

> "It's a simple question with a complicated answer I'm afraid. If you mean taking an existing, successful business and preparing it to launch into the franchise market, the answer is that it can be anything from a few thousand pounds to provide them with some basic information including some templates and limited guidance, to £30k+ to provide the full development service where we largely do all the work for them leaving them to concentrate on continuing to grow their core business.
>
> In addition to this they will need to think about costs for a Franchise Agreement (the legal contract) which is typically about

£4–5k, and marketing for franchisees including a recruitment website and advertising for their franchise opportunity. You will see it is not a cheap way to expand a business but after the system is all set up and running they will then be expanding using other people's money (their franchisees' investment)."

 www.thefranchisingcentre.com

 @franchisecentre

With the business set up as a franchise, you may be wondering about the financial return. Here's a summary of the amounts charged by three of the franchise businesses covered in this section.

FRANCHISE	COST OF FRANCHISE
Pyjama Drama	*Initial investment (franchise fee): £7,950 plus VAT* *Ongoing marketing levy: 2% of monthly turnover plus VAT* *Ongoing management fee: 8% of monthly turnover plus VAT*
Raring2Go	*Three bands of costs based on the number of primary age school children in the area.* *£13,995 – Over 25k pupils* *£11,995 – between 15k and 25k pupils* *£9,995 – up to 15k pupils*
Riverford	*£12,500 plus £8,500 training fee and 3% of retail sales paid as management service fee*

Having started in the 1980s, Riverford has become one of the most financially successful franchises in the UK.

Name: Nicky Morgan

Business: Riverford

26 years ago Guy Watson was a farmer with a field looking for ways to distribute his fruit and veg in Devon and decided upon a weekly veg box delivery service. Starting with 30 local orders, Riverford now serves over 60,000 homes across the UK. Soon after launch, Guy was receiving orders from London and realised a model would have to be created where customers were served by someone with greater local knowledge, as opposed to everything being managed from Devon.

"It worked!" says franchise manager, Nicky Morgan. "As we continued to receive enquiries from customers in other areas we didn't cover, we developed a sustainable, replicable business model. We chose the franchising route to expedite the development of our delivery network."

The company now grows produce at four farms located in different parts of the country from which produce is delivered to regional hubs. Franchisees do a daily collection from the hub and then deliver boxes to their customers.

Franchisees have sales targets set out in an annually agreed business plan and get help from Riverford HQ in meeting targets via orders generated from the main website. Riverford defines a franchise as a territory with a clear geographical set of postcode sectors. The cost for a new territory is £12,500 plus an initial £8,500 training fee and an ongoing contribution of 3% of weekly sales as a management service fee to head office. Taking this into account, the company does offer figures showing franchises who make 250 deliveries each week could make a profit of £23,000 in their first year of trading, after taking into account costs of the fee, a vehicle, marketing and salary. The company has 70 franchisees, covering 90 territories, i.e. equal to plentiful amounts of fruit and veg being delivered!

 **www.riverford.co.uk**

 **@riverford**

The legal bit

In making your business model available for sale as a franchise, you will want to know the legal contract between you and the franchisee is robust. Graeme Payne is a lawyer and franchise specialist and outlines the key points to be included in an agreement.

A well-drafted franchise agreement will include these points:

- Parties – will the franchisor set up a new company for the franchise business? Will the franchisee be a sole trader or limited liability company and if the latter will personal guarantees be provided?
- Protection of the franchisor's brand, know-how, confidential information, systems and processes;

- Obligations (both initial and ongoing) – scope of franchisor's and scope of franchisee's including franchise business system requirements;
- Financial obligations of franchisee to franchisor;
- Promotion of the brand by franchisor and franchisee;
- Ongoing monitoring by the franchisor and reporting requirements on the franchisee;
- Termination rights for the franchisor based on conduct or omissions by the franchisee;
- Non-competition requirements on franchisees – both during and after the term of the agreement;
- Disclosure obligations;
- Sale and purchase of the franchisee's business;
- Exclusion and limitation of the franchisor's liability to the franchisee.

Graeme Payne is a franchise lawyer with Bird & Bird LLP and provides a full range of legal services to franchisors.

 www.twobirds.com

 @twobirds

Name: Freddie St. George

Business: Raring2go!

Freddie St. George got into franchising and Raring2go! by acquiring the business from another franchisor in 2008. The original founder is still with the company, now as a franchisee, producing local magazines for parents looking at what to do and where to go with their children. The company has 50 franchisees doing the same across 56 territories in the UK.

"We look for people who recognise they are buying a business and not a salary; individuals who appreciate that with hard work, commitment, dedication, some sacrifice and application, success and financial freedom can be theirs. We are looking for people who have the get-up-and-go to make a home-based franchise business like Raring2go! work. Someone who has sales and marketing experience, a personable nature, demonstrates drive, ambition and determination and sees that the Raring2go! franchise means they are in business for themselves but not by themselves."

Franchisees pay £10,000 to £14,000 for the opportunity of buying into a tried and tested business format. For this, they receive an exclusive territory, operating manual, legal agreements, training in all aspects of running the business, a pre-loaded computer, stationery pack, branded merchandise and their own local revenue-generating website.

"We provide Continuing Professional Development training in all aspects of their business and our franchisee support team provide full head office support round the clock, on hand at all times during the working day to answer any query."

Franchisees generate revenue from local advertising in the magazine. They also have their own website which delivers an income from banners, sponsor opportunities and paid-for listings. Raring2go! does not take any percentage of advertising revenue from print or online sales.

With this model, Freddie is focused on increasing market share in the UK and finding more top quality people to join a growing group that does what it says in the company name.

 **www.raring2go.co.uk**

 **@raring2gohq**

Finding the perfect match

As much as a franchisee will ask questions of you and the business model, you will want to be sure they are the right fit for your brand and company. Spend time with any potential franchisee and ask yourself if you would be happy with this person representing your brand and the business you have built.

In asking the franchisors profiled here what they look for when recruiting franchisees, the factors most often cited were:

- Passion for the product
- Willingness to work hard and be part of a team
- Enthusiasm to learn how to start and grow a business
- Existing sales and marketing skills

The same applies to Phil and Clare Moran who are always on the lookout for the ideal consultants for their business, My Secret Kitchen.

Name: Clare Moran

Business: My Secret Kitchen

Husband and wife team, Phil and Clare Moran, started their food-tasting party business, My Secret Kitchen, in 2007 and have grown to the point where they now have over 300 consultants. For £99, consultants receive a Business Kit and a course of 12 training modules to help them get going in hosting tasting parties and selling the My Secret Kitchen range of products, for which consultants receive a commission.

"The first three parts of the training course are focused on start-up to launch and we offer these as a one-to-one phone session on a free conference line. Each comes with a workbook and are either run with our training and support team or more usually with the new consultant's team leader. Following that initial training, we have a same-day response service for any consultant queries via a dedicated email and phone service. The free conference line is also used for monthly meetings with our leaders plus new product training sessions that we record and put on the consultant forum and closed Facebook group for consultants."

The most successful consultants, in Clare's view, are those who are passionate about food, enjoy spending time with people, and want to give business a go. The company has recruited most of its new consultants through existing tasting events.

"In this setting the new consultant really gets to see the way the business is run. We also promote ourselves through social media and recommendations from the consultants themselves, i.e. word of mouth. We have had good press coverage through editorials and have attended large trade shows and events."

The company has a management team of five with three support team members working on a part-time basis. Together, the team has a clear vision to grow and a desire to see their products reach all corners of the UK.

"The downturn has meant we have needed to be flexible and respond to the environment but our passion and love of our products is as vibrant as ever. As long as we continue to share our foods with as many people as possible and make them as happy as possible, then we are happy too."

 www.mysecretkitchen.co.uk

 @mysecretkitchen

Is it a franchise or direct selling?

You may have spotted that the cost of becoming a My Secret Kitchen consultant is much smaller than the franchise fee paid to companies such as Riverford and Raring2go! This highlights the difference between franchise and direct selling which are close in nature.

In making the decision as to whether you want to grow through franchise or direct selling, be guided by a distinction made by direct-selling specialist, Dr Stewart Brodie.

> "Conventional business format franchising seldom involves initial investments of less than £20,000. Direct-selling mini franchises in comparison, are typically operated on a part-time basis. A minimum of capital outlay or legal process is involved, making for very low barriers to entry."[1]

Essentially, direct selling costs less than a franchise for the franchisee or consultant and involves them working, usually in a sales capacity, on a part-time basis as opposed to a franchisee who is likely to commit full-time to building their business.

As with franchising, direct selling is becoming more popular as a route for people to enter self-employment. The Direct Selling Association report found particular increases in the number of young people buying into direct-selling opportunities with a rise of 29% in 2012, leading to a total of 75,000 of the 400,000 direct sellers in the UK being under the age of 25. In an age of pressure to pay back student loans, young people are clearly looking for opportunities to earn in their spare time, which offers you and

1 Direct Sales Franchises in the UK: A Self-Employment Grey Area (ftp://ns1.ystp.ac.ir/YSTP/3/E-%20Book2%20%28G%29/E-%20book/Small%20Business/61.PDF)

your business a clear opportunity to perfect the model and make it available as a self-employment business opportunity for others.

Useful links

All the business owners profiled stressed the importance of accessing professional advice and support. Here are places to find it.

Industry bodies

British Franchise Association – the undisputed trade body for the franchise industry offering a wealth of information including links to banks that offer specialist franchise funding, franchise advisers and qualified solicitors. There's also a guide on how to franchise your business (**www.thebfa.org/franchise-your-business**) and seminars across the UK (**www.thebfa.org/franchise-seminars**) where you hear direct from the experts. Raise your profile and secure prizes through entering the industry awards (**www.thebfa.org/franchise-awards**) and consider joining the Association to give franchisees confidence as you're part of the national trade body.

 **www.thebfa.org**

 **@bfa_uk**

Encouraging Women into Franchising – an organisation created to do what the name implies and encourage more women into becoming a franchisee or franchise their own business. EWIF provides free advice to female business owners as well as a directory of qualified consultants and professionals.

 **www.ewif.org**

 **@EWIF1**

Direct Selling Association – in existence since 1965, the DSA represents the interests of, and promotes, direct-selling companies. Members include Avon, Temple Spa, Pampered Chef and Neal's Yard Remedies. This trade body puts on educational events, promotes direct selling in the media and hosts annual awards.

 www.dsa.org.uk

 @DSAUK

Events

The Franchise Show – an annual event focused on people interested in becoming franchisees. Attend as an observer to start with, before becoming one of the available franchise options!

 www.thefranchiseshow.co.uk

 @franchiseshowuk

Publications

The Franchise Magazine

 www.thefranchisemagazine.net

 @thefranchisemag

Franchise World

 www.franchiseworld.co.uk

 @franchiseworldm

The Networked Venture

It's not strictly a franchise but a model I'm seeing take off is the 'network model' which involves similar principles to franchising in the careful selection and training of self-employed agents who represent your brand. You don't hire staff full-time but do bring together a collection of talented and highly-qualified individuals to service sizeable contracts.

It's a model I'm convinced we will see develop across more markets and sectors. There are a few key elements to it:

- **Founding team** – who have the vision to create a business based on a small and nimble central team, with work outsourced to an army of professionals.
- **Quality workforce** – with a rigorous selection process and ongoing training in place so the company attracts and retains prestigious clients.
- **Effective communications** – ensuring the workforce is able to communicate with each other and the client is made aware of project development too.
- **Single mission** – with management and the network of freelance professionals working towards a common goal.

It's a route to growing a business that is working for Time etc profiled on page 10 and, in the PR industry, The PR Network.

Name: **Nicky Imrie**

Business: **The PR Network**

With strong backgrounds working in corporate PR, Nicky Imrie and Georgina Blizzard set up The PR Network in 2005 as 50/50 shareholders. The company has grown into a management team of four with a managing director and second director now having a share in the business.

This team may run the business day-to-day but client work is delivered by a talented army of PR professionals, located across the globe and with expertise across different disciplines. Best of all? These associates are all self-employed and self-motivated individuals who come together to service contracts for major brands, creating a model for Nicky and George that means growth comes without being slowed by employment legislation and the associated costs of hiring full-time. The talent they are hiring isn't too keen on being on the payroll either; they want the freedom and flexibility that comes with being their own boss, combined with being part of a big team.

As the two founders say on the company website: 'Nicky and George had a vision to create a new type of PR business based on the globe's best freelance talent and supported by a central hub. That's The PR Network.'

Nicky explains:

"We have grown the network predominantly on a referral basis, so freelance associates are recommended by senior people we know and trust. All applicants go through a rigorous joining process and have to meet strict criteria if they are to be accepted into the network."

Once associates have been accepted, they work to a set of templates and methodologies that have been developed based on the management team's years of experience working for the UK's best PR agencies. There are ongoing training courses on subjects such as social media so associates can maintain a level of CPD (Continuous Professional Development) even though they are now working independently.

"We publish regular associate newsletters, hold biannual get-togethers, and have a private LinkedIn group for associates where we share industry updates and network news. We work flexibly from a range of locations: home offices, private members' clubs and co-working spaces in London where the whole team can get together for meetings and collaborative working. We also provide informal support to our associates to help them develop and maintain their freelance careers."

It's an arrangement that works well for clients. The PR Network takes a detailed brief from the prospective client and then takes into account a range of factors such as sector experience, location, budget, culture and chemistry to choose the associates that best suit the job.

"We know all our associates so once we have the brief, we can match that with the associate or associate team who will be the best fit with the client."

Head office secures the contracts and then pays associates to deliver the work, supported and managed by a member of The PR Network management team. To the client, it is seamless and cost-effective.

"We give our associates a mix of tools and services so they feel and act like a cohesive team. Many of our PR accounts have several associates working together as a virtual team, often in different countries, so collaboration tools such as Skype and Yammer are essential for effective communication. We also offer conference call facilities and face-to-face meeting facilities for London-based associates to get together and brainstorm client campaigns. Associates get the benefits of working for themselves with the support structure of a bigger organisation."

With a roster of clients including Apple, Adobe, Zipcar and Mastercard, the company has gone global. These major brands require work to be carried out across borders and this has carried The PR Network into new territories with an international network developing and associates being found through tapping into the existing network. Continuing to serve these global clients is high on the list of priorities for the next 12 months, as is extending the service beyond pure PR into broader communications and content marketing.

"We have spent eight years as a well-kept secret," says Nicky. "We have focused on building a fantastic network of talented professionals and acquiring a stellar client base. Now it's time to promote the concept and generate more opportunities for our associates so the Network can continue to grow."

 **www.theprnetwork.co.uk**

 **@prnetwork**

With your sector and scope of service decided, creating a networked business involves having the right training, client

approach and foundations in place but then growing at speed as a workforce of self-employed individuals take a vested interest in seeing the company succeed. In 'Keeping it legal' on page 177 we look at the type of legal contracts to have in place to ensure the relationship between you and your freelancers is a watertight one.

Productise

Take your product, service or skill and put it in a box. Customers will buy your product and pay a higher amount for the original item, i.e. you!

In 2009 I went on a business road trip of the UK and met an entrepreneur who was making high style dresses. Her issue, she explained, was that one dress took eight to ten hours to make and she was struggling to keep up with demand whilst holding down a day job. The solution? She decided to make kits, putting base materials for the dress in a box with DIY instructions. I thought this was inspired. It took only 30 minutes to put a box together so you could make and sell 20 kits in the time it would take to make one dress. In doing so, you are offering the customer an experience and the pleasure of making their own dress, based on your instructions, and as the finished item is likely to be photographed/blogged/tweeted, customers act as your marketing agents too. It was this meeting that convinced me of the value of productising and putting what you do in a box.

This is one of the ways Enterprise Nation has grown. Our first book, *Spare Room Start Up*, was released in 2008 and since then we have published over 50 books, eBooks and kits to package up small business knowledge and expertise (mine and others) so this can be made available for sale or free to customers. This has contributed to the growth of the business and, most importantly, has meant thousands of people have been able to access this knowledge at an affordable cost and apply it to start and grow their own business.

Digital products

Let's first look at how to create digital products to enhance and grow your business. This applies whether you are selling a physical or knowledge based item. Taking the examples of a business owner making cushions and another designing logos, this is how it works:

PRODUCT	CUSHION MAKER	LOGO DESIGNER
eBook	*Author '25 cushion patterns for the ideal home'*	*Author 'The most famous logos in history'*
Webinar	*Present on how to make a cushion in less than an hour*	*Present on logo design for beginners*
E-learning course	*Deliver 'Cushion making in 10 steps'*	*Deliver '10 things to do with your logo'*
Podcast	*Record 'Cushion making at coffee time'*	*Record 'Logos at lunch – a daily tip for getting your logo to market'*
App	*Create 'Snap & Craft' which enables customers to photograph a cushion and download the closest pattern template to make it*	*Create 'Love your logo' which enables people to take pictures of their favourite logos and create a mood board for their own creation.*

You get the idea. You are taking your knowledge, boxing it up, selling it to clients and growing your business and profile as an expert. Once you have created an eBook, webinar, app or e-learning course, it's out there in the market and generating sales so you can move onto the next project, i.e. you make the product once and it's available for many people to buy. This enables your business to scale without being too dependent on your time and, what's more, you can create these products without even leaving the home office! I'll show you how.

eBooks

Become a published author by writing an eBook (print books are covered on page 63) on your specialist subject. Here are the five steps to go about it:

- Subject
- Write
- Format
- Publish
- Promote

Subject – decide the topic and title for your eBook. This will be determined by your target audience and what you'd like them to take from it. The bestselling eBooks on Enterprise Nation are *50 ways to find funding for your business* and *49 quick ways to market your business for free* – you can tell from this that people like clear titles that show what's inside!

Write – give yourself quiet time and space to write but do make a start! You may even consider hiring the services of an editor or copywriter to help (see 'Top 10 sites on which to find the talent you're after' on page 168 for details) but I think it's better to write books and eBooks yourself as the text will be in your own 'voice'. If you go with a publisher, a professional editor will review your work. In terms of length, eBooks tend to be 20,000 words and best written in Word or Pages on a Mac.

Format – from the basic document, format the eBook for Kindle and iBooks so it can be uploaded and sold via the powerful platforms of Amazon, Apple and Kobo. On Amazon, you can be selling in 24 hours but with iBooks it can take four to six weeks for your eBook to be approved so be sure to build this into your promotion timetable.

Publish – your options are to self-publish or go with a publisher – see a comparison table below. Should you decide to self-publish, use platforms such as Lulu (www.lulu.com/publish/ebooks), Blurb (www.blurb.co.uk/business) or Smashwords (www.smashwords.com) which guide you through the process and provide the tools needed to publish and promote your masterpiece. If you're approaching a publisher, follow the advice of Alex Johnson on page 64 and Ed Faulkner on page 66.

SELF-PUBLISH	GO WITH PUBLISHER
You write and edit (or hire a pro)	*You write and publisher edits*
You/pro design (including cover) and upload to platforms	*Publisher designs and uploads*
You source your own ISBN	*The publisher assigns your ISBN*
You own rights to the content	*The publisher has exclusive rights while the contract is in place*
You keep all the sales proceeds (taking into account that if the eBook is on eBook platforms, they take a slice and may restrict your RRP)	*You receive a royalty on each sale (taking into account that if the eBook is on eBook platforms, they take a slice too)*
You promote	*You promote!*

"If you are going to self-publish, invest in your professional team and find an editor as well as a cover designer to help you create the best product possible for your reader."

JOANNA PENN, FOUNDER, THE CREATIVE PENN,
www.thecreativepenn.com

Promote – with the eBook published, work begins. Promote the finished product to your own network and clients, via complementary blogs, to corporate contacts who could be interested in multiple downloads and across the major platforms (shown below). The more eBooks downloaded, the more income you generate (if a price has been set) and the more of an authority on the topic you become.

*"There are many opportunities for authors to promote themselves on eBook platforms, including being part of the Kindle Owners' Lending Library, on-site and newsletter promotions, and the Kindle Daily Deal on Amazon as well as being part of the Amazon Author Central network (***authorcentral.amazon.com***)."*

LOUISE MILES, FORMER COMMISSIONING EDITOR, BRIGHTWORD PUBLISHING

PLATFORM	REACH & REVENUE
Amazon Building your Book for Kindle: kdp.amazon.com/self-publishing/help?topicId=A2MB3WT2D0PTNK Kindle Direct Publishing kdp.amazon.com/self-publishing/signin	*Make your eBook available to Kindle readers and Amazon customers. It takes 24 hours for your eBook to be uploaded and you earn up to 70% royalty on each sale.*
iTunes iTunes 'Frequently Asked Questions' for publishers www.apple.com/itunes/content-providers/book-faq.html	*Claiming 130 million downloads in March 2013, this is a powerful platform to be on. You earn 70% royalty on each sale and can upload your eBook via the iTunes Producer.*
Kobo www.kobo.com/writinglife	*3.5 million eBooks and readers in 190 countries. There is no cost to upload but there's a fee to pay if you use Kobo Publisher to convert your text into a Kobo eBook.*

Take into account the time it will take to set up bookselling accounts as you need to supply personal details, bank transfer information for payments as well as read and sign contracts/user agreements, etc.

Francesca Geens decided to box up her knowledge of IT services and consulting and this has resulted in happier clients and a more robust customer database.

Name: Francesca Geens

Business: Digital Dragonfly

Francesca's company, Digital Dragonfly, provides IT services for solo business owners.

"There is an increasing trend for people to leave corporate jobs and set up on their own as freelancers and consultants. These businesses are often home-based or very mobile and have very specific technology requirements. I wanted to set up a business that catered specifically to the tech needs of this niche. It's the basic but ever so important things like backup, syncing your devices, sharing data with associates, productivity apps, mobile working, cloud services and hardware where I can help."

Francesca has quickly become an expert in this area; paying clients were able to access this expertise but Francesca wanted to share her knowledge further, to raise her profile and attract more clients. Writing an eBook was a route to achieving this.

"Writing the eBook was very time-consuming but it needed to be done. I think it's really important to make high-quality information available as a way to show your expertise, your approach and how you work with clients. It also allows me to capture email addresses and start engaging with potential clients through my newsletter as well as reaching out to a larger audience by using social media as a tool to spread the link."

The eBook, *The Ultimate Guide to Technology for Independent Professionals*, has successfully raised Francesca's profile, attracted more people onto her database and enhanced her reputation as the expert in this field –raising the price clients are willing to pay to access the expert herself. As a next stage in the 'productise' process, Francesca's goal is to box up her skills into a monthly subscription model, encouraging clients to sign up to a recurring plan.

"Until now I have relied on project work which requires a steady stream of clients but to scale up I need to crack the monthly model and this is what I am testing at the moment. Once I have that solved I plan to bring on a freelance techie to free up more of my time to create new products and take it from there."

 **www.digitaldragonfly.co.uk**

 **@f_dragonfly**

Ask the Author

I asked three recent authors of Enterprise Nation eBooks as to what they thought the benefits were of publishing your own eBook.

"Well-written eBooks provide an excellent platform to position yourself or your company as an authority or expert within your given field of expertise. eBooks which can be downloaded for free from your website in exchange for basic contact information (an email address) also help you build your email marketing list and provide a fantastic lead generation tool for business."

John Hayes, author of *A Crash Course in Email Marketing*

"It enables you to reach a wider audience – nationally and globally."

Emily Coltman, author of *Very Awkward Tax*

"Now when I take on freelance projects it's immediately recognised that I know what I'm talking about. I'm viewed as an expert in what I do and am treated as such. I find it intriguing that collecting work together into a volume can have such a profound effect, but it's helped my business no end."

Rachael Oku, author of *Become a Freelance Writer*

Online learning/E-learning

Create an online learning course about your skill and deliver this to an invited audience. There are two ways you can do this:

- Via your own site – using online learning technologies
- Via a dedicated e-learning site

Or maybe a combination of both!

The technologies you can deploy on your own site to present your expertise include platforms such as Blackboard where you create a virtual classroom (**www.blackboard.com**, **@blackboardemea**), GoToWebinar which enables you to invite up to 500 people to hear and/or watch you present (**www.gotowebinar.com**, **@GoToWebinar**) and CoveritLive that acts as a live chat facility (**www.coveritlive.com**, **@coveritlive**).

"Blackboard has proved to be a robust e-learning system for Creative University online courses. It is flexible, reliable and has interactive functions that allow our students and instructors to communicate and learn. The discussion boards, blogs and interactive grade centre are the most popular areas of the courses and add value to more static course materials."

AME VERSO, CONTENT MANAGER, F+W MEDIA INTERNATIONAL AND THE CREATIVE UNIVERSITY

The websites on which you can deliver courses include:

- **CreativeLive** – founded in 2010 to enable artists and entrepreneurs to deliver workshops on photography, video, design, business, audio, music, and software training (www.creativelive.com, @creativelive)
- **eHow** – videos displayed on this site are made available for free but it could be a useful test bed to trial your content (www.ehow.co.uk, @ehowuk)
- **YouTube** – create your own channel and secure advertising to fund the cost (www.youtube.com, @youtube)

For an email-based elearning course, look at Mailchimp (www.mailchimp.com). This is the tool we use at Enterprise Nation to deliver a 12-week StartUp course to thousands of people. It was easy to set up and is now automated so learners receive their lessons on time and in their inbox. San Sharma managed the process:

> "If you're a paying customer of MailChimp, you can send a series of automatic messages to people who sign up on your website. It's a feature called autoresponders, and it's a great way to follow up with visitors after they've done something on your site, like place an order, or – as we've done – signed up for an educational series.
>
> When readers sign up for our Startup Course they get a new business lesson each week for 12 weeks, sent to their inboxes. The beauty of it – for us – is that we spent some time, before we launched the course, loading the 12 business lessons into MailChimp; we put a sign-up form on our website; the rest is completely automated."

Deliver training and charge people for attending using GoToTraining (**www.gototraining.com**), which is online training software allowing you to hold unlimited interactive training sessions with up to 200 people. With this tool you can reach out to students and potential customers across the globe (without having to travel), make tests and materials available online, and introduce audio and video conferencing into the training too.

Value of Video

To deliver content via tools such as Blackboard, you just need access to the internet and a webcam. Developing and delivering your own online course is likely to require the services of a videographer. Find them on the talent marketplaces profiled in 'Top 10 sites on which to find the talent you're after' on page 168.

Julie Hall is growing her business, Women Unlimited, through making the most of new technologies to share content with fee-paying audiences.

Name: Julie Hall

Business: Women Unlimited

When Julie Hall launched Women Unlimited in September 2008, the plan was to create an online magazine where women could learn from other people's business experiences.

"We started doing webinars after a couple of years as it was a great way to connect with our growing audience, without people having to physically make the effort to attend an event. I love doing live stuff as I think the energy is very different. Google Hangouts, a live video feature on Google Plus, have become a staple product of what I do as they are an exciting way of connecting with both the people I interview and giving the audience the chance to watch live."

As Google Hangouts are immediately uploaded to YouTube, this opens up Julie's content to an even larger audience and with the Hangouts run via a web browser and webcam, they don't require any extra software.

"Businesses can run Hangouts which are public and allow anyone to participate or you can run ones where only invited people can watch. There are so many ways this technology can be used such as live Q&A sessions, interviews, training, marketing and customer service. I think it's a really exciting technology."

Julie applies her own advice when it comes to promoting Hangouts and online courses across the web. She turns to social media and has a strong presence on the platforms that are most popular with her clients.

"Social media requires regular interaction to be successful so I usually suggest starting out with your favourite social media platform as you will already be familiar and participating. If you are moving into a new one, spend a couple of weeks observing and watching other people to see what works. Once you have mastered one channel, move onto another."

Julie charges for programmes, using free content as a way of showing customers the value of what they would receive if they upgraded to paying status.

"I'm a great believer in making the free stuff as good as our paid stuff. The bulk of our revenue comes from online courses, affiliate commissions on other people's courses and our monthly business clubs."

Julie plans to grow this revenue and the business by expanding into new towns and cities across the UK. You can guarantee she'll be making the most of technology each step of the way.

 **www.womenunlimitedworldwide.com**

 **@women_unlimited**

Apps

Find talented app makers on the marketplaces profiled on page 168 who can turn your knowledge into a downloadable tool for customers and hopefully their networks too.

Physical products

In addition to creating digital products, move into the physical world. Place your knowledge in a physical box and head out to events, trade shows, markets and PopUps. Let's return to our example of the cushion maker and logo designer and consider their options to keep growing.

PRODUCT	CUSHION MAKER	LOGO DESIGNER
Print book	*Publish 'Classic cushions over the ages; the history of cushion making'*	*Publish 'Living logos: design concepts behind the world's most famous brands'*
DIY kit	*Create a box set of textiles and a DIY pattern set of instructions to follow*	*Create a box set of templates, colour wheels and fonts with instructions to follow*
Events	*Host events on 'How to make your own cushion'*	*Host events on 'How to design your own logo'*
Speaking engagements	*Speak at other people's events that draw a crowd of your ideal customers*	*Speak at other people's events that draw a crowd of your ideal customers*

Print books

Print is far from dead. The British Publishers Association confirmed sales of print books worth £3bn in 2013 – this may be down on previous years but it's certainly not out. Writing and publishing a print book gets you on the shelves, in view, and hopefully a little more in profit.

Alex Johnson has turned his blog about shedworking into not one but two books.

Name: Alex Johnson

Business: Shedworking

Journalist and blogger Alex Johnson had been writing his Shedworking blog, a lifestyle guide for shedworkers, for two years before it went from online into print.

"I never had any strong intention of turning the blog into a book. In fact, I mildly disliked the trend of blog-to-book, partly because I think most blogs don't readily lend themselves to books.

It was reading about a new publishing company – The Friday Project – that got me interested. They specialised in blogs-to-books and other interesting 21st century ways of publishing so I sent them a brief enquiry about the possibility of a shedworking book. They said yes almost immediately. But just as it was about to be published, they were swallowed up by a major publishing house which after some umming and ahhhing decided not to go ahead with it. I then contacted about a dozen more publishers and half a dozen agents, all of whom were very positive about it but none said yes. I was right on the point of giving up when a friend placed a book with Frances Lincoln – who do a lot of books about gardening and architecture – and I thought if they won't take it then nobody will. Luckily they were very keen from the start and it ended up being a very happy marriage."

Alex wrote a proposal that was sent to the publishers and was helped in the process by a polite but firm friend.

"I showed the proposal to a journalist and author friend of mine – Emma Townshend, who writes a lot about gardening. She was very polite about it but also said it didn't sell the book well enough. I'm not by nature a big shouty person about my own abilities so this was very helpful and I incorporated all of her suggestions. It was certainly much better as a result. Having spoken to other authors since I'd say that the most important thing to do is show how your book will fill a gap in the market – publishers in my experience are decent people and interested in intriguing ideas of any kind, even very niche ones like my two, but they also don't want to lose money so you need to present them with something that is likely to sell – a couple of publishers turned down the Bookshelf book on that basis, even though they liked the idea (and while it's not sold like Harry Potter, it has sold over 25,000 copies worldwide so that underlines another tip that you should believe in your project even if other professionals aren't so sure). Also mention your social media presence as this indicates that you already have an interested market in what you do."

With two books now out on the market, Alex says it's hard to quantify the financial benefits to the business but being a published author has certainly added some prestige to what he does.

"The knock-on effect is that I've been asked to write articles, comment on radio and television (I was on BBC Breakfast when the Shedworking book came out which was a hoot). And of course while I haven't sold enough to retire from the proceeds, they do bring money in, especially the second one for which I also got a decent advance. In terms of advertising, having a couple of books out certainly helps to persuade potential advertisers that I'm serious about what I do and that its quality has been recognised quite widely."

There could be more works in the pipeline from this author as his publisher has suggested a new idea to Alex.

"I suppose this shows that once you have your foot in the door, it's much easier to go about getting more books published."

 **www.shedworking.co.uk**

 **@shedworking**

"As a business books publisher I am always on the lookout for inspirational business stories and practical advice that can help readers develop and improve their own businesses. Amidst all the 'noise' of the modern technological era we live in, people need experts and good advice more than ever, so I want to hear from authors who can genuinely offer something unique and useful. For me, the best business book pitches tell me something new, they have a distinctive 'voice' and they offer readers knowledge that will help them succeed in their own careers."

Ed Faulkner, Publishing Director, Virgin Books and Ebury Publishing

Be seen and heard

With an eBook or book on the market, do one extra step and go audio! If your book is selling well, you may receive an approach from audio book publishers who ask for the rights to produce an audio version but if you'd prefer to take matters in your own hands, read the blog post on this topic from self-publishing expert Joanna Penn's website, The Creative Penn (**www.thecreativepenn.com/2013/03/06/audiobook**). With the audio book produced, upload (and sell) via platforms such as Audible (**www.audible.co.uk**).

"Typically an author signs over audio rights with the print and eBook contracts and it is then up to the publisher to invest in producing the audio version. If authors own the rights to their audio and have it recorded independently, they can act as their own publisher."

Chris Book, Former CEO, Bardowl

Events

Demonstrate your expertise in person by hosting events and workshops. The beauty of this is that customers pay to attend and pick up your tips whilst also hopefully buying your product and becoming a loyal customer. These three entrepreneurs show how it can be achieved, whether you're training is in sewing, photography, or baking bread!

Name: **Arianna Cadwallader**

Business: **Saturday Sewing Session**

Starting with one sewing class on a Saturday, Arianna Cadwallader has increased her range and regularity of events so they are now being held every weeknight bar Friday and across the weekend. When asked about the most popular classes, Arianna replies:

"Cushions cushions cushions! Dressmaking is also seeing a massive revival as are our Make do and Mend sessions. They focus on altering and upcycling items you have had in your wardrobe for ages. By learning a few simple techniques there is no need to send your trousers to be hemmed ever again or throw away something because it's too big."

As well as increasing the number of events, Arianna has had to change the location since launch:

"Just over a year after sewing sessions started, we upped sticks and moved from the gorgeous upstairs of the Chelsea Ram pub, where we held classes every Saturday, to a studio just down the street in Chelsea. It enabled us to open up lots more sewing sessions and as a maker and milliner, my old studio was in my flat and I was getting a bit tight on space. So scarily but wonderfully, we combined the two and I took the step to get a proper working studio that could be used for both businesses. I do my designs and makes in the day and then the studio opens up in the evening to people who want to learn to sew.

It has been a wonderful few years. It's amazing what working hard, late nights, energy, tea and naivety can achieve! I have no idea where the time has gone and how things have changed. I loved doing the classes above the pub but I don't miss lugging the machines up two flights of stairs or hearing the football chanting in the pub below, however I have a massive fondness and appreciation for the people who helped me plant those first few seeds to make this business grow. I love where we are now and feel really lucky that the business is working and growing. There was a feeling at the time of a sewing revival and I think we started the business at a perfect time. Now with *The Sewing Bee* and other sewing-related shows it helps our business without a doubt.

In the next 12 months we are looking at working on our marketing, hopefully getting some videos out there and we are starting to make pattern kits for people to do in their own time. We are also looking to train up a couple more teachers so I can step away from the teaching side. Although I feel totally blessed in the people I have met in the sessions, my workload is getting bigger so I will be continuing 'behind the scenes' alongside working on my own millinery/making business. Cripes... It's going to be busy. Fun, but busy."

 **www.saturdaysewingsession.co.uk**

 **@AriannaLondon**

Name: Alex Gooch

Business: Artisan baker

"I started putting on courses in 2012. People had been asking me to run them for four or five years and I'd always wanted to but never managed to find the time – not that I exactly have the time now either!

There is something very satisfying about teaching the simple beauty of bread. I run courses in my own bakery in Hay-on-Wye and at cookery schools, such as the Chef's Room at Blaenavon, near Abergavenny. The people who attend one course often go on to do all of them. I stay in contact with them and am always available for advice and information.

Once expenses are deducted, I don't make a huge amount of money from the courses alone but it's good marketing and a great experience interacting with my customers and getting to know them better.

I run the courses myself but in the background I'm helped by my staff and family to organise and administer them. We're about to get even busier as we have many more planned over the next 12 months."

 **www.alexgoochbaker.com**

Name: Sarah J. Thomas

Business: Sarah J. Thomas Photography

"I've always been an advocate for specialising in a certain area of photography rather than spreading your time too thinly between genres such as children, portraits, weddings, etc. It's always been my opinion that being a specialist in your field is essential and that the skills required for wedding photography (for example) are very different to those of a child photographer. Yes, technically it doesn't matter but the people skills, marketing and branding are very different beasts. I do however see the value in diversifying your business and developing your specialist brand. This is where the idea for my photography classes evolved from. Designed initially as training courses to teach parents to take better pictures of their children, the course has organically grown to encompass bloggers, small business owners and general hobbyists. My beginners' classes are designed to encourage people to have the confidence to get their camera off auto mode and to explain the basic principles of how the camera works.

At the moment I host a beginner's photography workshop every two months. As a sole trader I need to be able to run the courses to compliment my main area of work and not to compete with it. I carefully manage my schedule to run a higher number of classes in the slower periods of the year. As an on location photographer this tends to be over the winter months.

When I first had the idea to run classes people around me were a little surprised and concerned that it would be a mistake. After all, why teach people to do what you do? Would it lose me business? Would people choose to take photos themselves rather than commission me? To be honest these concerns have not been an issue. People generally want to use their camera to capture the everyday moments, not to create professional portraits. By teaching people the basics it has gained me more business as trainees have more understanding of what I do and the challenges I face in my day-to-day work. Many of my trainees have commissioned me for family portrait sessions after coming on a course. Previous customers have also attended my courses, which is wonderful.

So far I have used basic forms of marketing to generate interest in the courses such as my website (**www.essentialcameraskills.co.uk**), social media, email marketing, direct contact with previous customers and a little local press. I have been careful not to go all guns blazing when marketing the classes as they run quite infrequently at the moment and I wanted to ensure I can meet demand.

The plan for the next 12 months is to continue with the beginner's workshops, enhance my marketing and slowly increase the number of courses scheduled over 2015. I am also being approached by people aspiring to start photography businesses of their own and fellow professional photographers looking to enhance their skills so they can host workshops and 1-2-1 training. This is a natural progression for me but will need careful planning. Come back to me in 12 months and I'll tell you all about it!"

www.sarahjthomas.com

www.essentialcameraskills.co.uk

@sarah_j_thomas

Here are the steps to putting on a workshop or face-to-face training that will deliver rave reviews:

1. **Invite** – promote the workshop to your existing community and network and across blogs, websites and media that you know attract your customers. Have a call to action, inviting people to register for a place via sites like Eventbrite (www.eventbrite.com) which enables you to track numbers and keep attendees updated. Choose a location that's your home office/kitchen/studio or by approaching someone with space that's not being utilised and who would appreciate the footfall.
2. **Delight** – inform and entertain attendees by demonstrating your skill. Take pictures to upload to social media platforms and consider recording the event for a live webcast or edited into future clips and used as a video-based learning course. Use Storify (www.storify.com) to collect tweets from the event and share on your site as a story for those unable to attend but keen to follow the script! After the event, follow up with attendees and keep in touch with a newsletter, offering deals and discounts for future events.

Agree to speak at other people's events and consider charging a speaker fee if you're playing a role in attracting paying customers or sponsors to the event.

Sell product in a PopUp

With product in hand, consider a PopUp to get your stock in more hands. PopUp Britain (**www.popupbritain.com**) was a project I launched in 2012 to open up empty shops and fill them with small businesses wanting to trade. The project continues under the leadership of the ATCM (Association of Town and City Management) and has been joined on the scene by PopUp platforms, We Are Pop Up (**www.wearepopup.com**) and Appear Here (**www.appearhere.co.uk**).

Alexandra van Berckel of luxury shoe brand Pinucci offers her view on the experience – and benefits – of testing a physical shop as a route to meeting customers, making sales, and being spotted by buyers.

"Part of the ethos of PopUp Britain is that we all sell each other's products as well as our own and in every store all the brands are encouraged to work together as a collaborative effort within the shared retail space – it is very much like how a department store works – and as we know, successful retail businesses depend on different teams working well with each other.

By meeting and building a rapport with other start-ups from a range of business and cultural backgrounds we have increased our network and many collaborations have developed.

We used the opportunity of popping up in Piccadilly to introduce key pieces from the spring/summer 2014 collection, which had been shown in Milan at a trade show but not yet shown to the public.

Being in Piccadilly was unique; where else can you get to speak with a buyer from Fortnum & Mason (who we're delighted to say loved our men's shoes) and meet DTZ, the corporate real estate and facilities management specialists – who suggested we were a great brand for Westfield – all on the same day? As a direct result of being in the store we are in discussions with a bespoke tailors and have been approached by a UK-wide menswear label looking to stock some of our new season's men's collection.

For Pinucci, discovering our customers and being discovered by customers is always a delight. With British and international customers coming in the shop across the week we are able to gauge which models (and colours) will be most popular because of the instant customer reaction and feedback. It's very exciting for us that we have a growing waiting list with lots of pre-orders for our new collection and we're delighted that the website is seeing a rise in unique visitors. We handed out more than 400 cards, lookbooks and postcards and it seems that people did then make the time to look us up."

 **www.pinucci.com**

 **@frompinucci**

Sales via subscription

Having wrapped up your product or service in a box, a further route to market is to introduce a membership or subscription scheme that sees customers sign up and receive your product each week/month/whenever they choose.

The subscription model is becoming increasingly popular as we discovered at a sell-out Enterprise Nation event in November 2014 featuring successful subscription businesses Hello Fresh, Weekend Box Club and HP's Instant Ink.

Two businesses profiled here that have decided to adopt this model are Jamsmith and Trinkets.

Name: Vicky Smith

Business: Jamsmith

Having started in autumn 2011, Vicky Smith is Mrs Jamsmith, testing and making beautiful preserves from her home kitchen in the Lake District. Before launching the business, Vicky did a lot of research to find a business model that would work around her location and family.

"The subscription model seemed perfect: I know each month how many jars I'm making, thus minimising wastage and being in a position to buy (or pick) exactly the seasonal fruit I need. I am in control of volumes through my waiting list, so can move forward at my own pace. I have developed some close relationships with customers through email chit-chat, some of whom have been ordering from me since I launched. I write a newsletter each month, explaining the provenance of the ingredients and why I've chosen the combination of flavours and in return I get useful feedback. I like the fun and control element I have with the subscription model. I don't supply shops at the moment (except sometimes my local farmshop with damson cheese) because my product yields/margins are small, although I do produce limited editions to order."

Customers are invited to join a one- or three-month Jamsmith monthly membership and receive two jars of jam, marmalade or fruit butter per month plus tasting notes, recipes and serving suggestions as well as news via the emails. One-month membership is £10, or it's £27 for three months.

Vicky labels, personalises, packages and posts all the jam herself.

"I have a good relationship with my local (very rural!) post office, but I am looking into the Royal Mail business package service and a fulfilment house is something to think about too!"

The feedback Vicky receives from customers is that people like the surprise of receiving a special treat every month and appreciate it's personalised for them.

Vicky doesn't currently offer subscription outside the UK, but does have customers abroad who buy for family within the UK.

"My 12-month plan is to refine my costs, admin and production methods without compromising quality; to develop my limited edition range; give more jam-making demonstrations; enter some quality food awards and attend one or two good retail events. I am also about to start working on a freelance basis for my local Chamber of Commerce, helping women in a similar situation to me start their food businesses."

It's set to be a busy time for the jam-maker who has chosen subscription as a route to growth.

 **www.jamsmith.co.uk**

 **@jamsmithclub**

Name: Genevieve Murphy

Business: Trinkets

Genevieve Murphy and business partner Kate Barry both had backgrounds working in technology companies, specifically on mobile content and delivery.

"We started at the beginning of mobile 1.0 in 2002 selling ringtones (in the days of the crazy frog!) and mobile content as subscription services. We knew and understood how the subscription model worked, so applied this to Trinkets. We thought a regular delivery of feminine care products was the most obvious and suitable subscription to offer. Launching a business model that you have experience and an understanding of has been critical to the development of the business."

The company sells tampons, pads and liners in stylish boxes that are delivered, on subscription, to your door.

"I think there has been a real surge in the past few years of subscription-based business. The beauty boxes have really made an impact with companies like Stylist Pick, Graze, Birchbox and of course the original subscription commerce success story, LoveFilm. It is a complex business model and you really have to understand the metrics behind how it works and what price you are paying to acquire each customer. Kate, my co-founder, is the numbers expert in our partnership and is genius at modelling the subscription basis of the business."

Following an early stage investment from one of the founders of LoveFilm, the company is now preparing a listing to fundraise via crowdfunding with Seedrs.

"The money will help us scale the business by investing in marketing and customer acquisition, product extension, and updates to our technology platform which we custom built. This investment will be the event to take Trinkets to the next level."

 **www.trinketwomen.com**

 **@trinketwomen**

'Funding' on page 223 onwards covers details on crowdfunding and other funding sources.

Secure a sponsor

In creating digital and physical products around your area of knowledge and expertise, you are creating valuable content. This is content that could be sponsored by big brands wanting to engage with your customers. For the final time, let us return to our cushion maker and logo designer to explore the approaches they could make.

	CUSTOMER COMMUNITY	**OF INTEREST TO**
Cushion maker	*Artisans and makers, interior designers, furnishings buyers*	*Brands selling home furnishings, paint, etc.*
Logo designer	*Graphic designers and early stage business owners*	*Brands selling tech, finance, insurance, home office set-up products and services*

What you offer a big brand sponsor is:

- A community of customers with whom they would like to engage
- Objectivity as you endorse their product as the respected voice in your sector
- Content for the big brand to share via their own website/social media/PR networks
- The excitement of being connected with a small, innovative and growing business

Work up a tailored proposal highlighting these benefits, include a cost (based on the level of your reach online and off) and send it to a marketing contact in the company – you can often find such contacts on the company website or on LinkedIn – or get in touch with their media and PR agency. The benefit to you in securing a sponsor is receiving income and the extra marketing firepower of the big brand promoting the project.

With the cost of producing and promoting the content covered by big brand sponsors, the money you make from selling content to consumers equals pure profit. It should be said that few of these products on their own are likely to make you sufficient income for a full-time living (unless, of course, you are JK Rowling!) but taken together they do add up.

PRODUCT	VOLUME PER ANNUM	INCOME PER ANNUM
Digital		
eBook	*500 sales x £3*	£1,500
Webinar	*Free to log on*	£0
E-learning course	*250 subscribers paying £40 each*	£10,000
App	*1,000 downloads at £2 each*	£2,000
Physical		
Physical book	*2,000 sales x £12*	£24,000
Events	*6 events with 30 people paying £30 each*	£5,400
Speaking engagement	*4 engagements with £500 fee each*	£2,000
Product via PopUp/PitchUp/ monthly subscription	*Dependent on cost of product. Taking Jamsmith subscription example, say 150 people x £10 per month*	*£1,500 per month, i.e. £18,000 per annum*
Total income for productising your knowledge (excluding income secured from sponsors)		**£62,900**

Shoo Rayner has become a master at the multiple income stream approach to business with his shed as the nerve centre of an international education empire.

Name: Shoo Rayner

Business: Shoo Rayner

"In the days before social media, I had a comfortable working pattern. My books would often be translated into minority languages (Finnish, Catalan, Walloon!) and other major languages around the world. I always kidded myself that I was a real business, but all I really had to do was keep coming up with ideas that publishers would like. I found a comfortable niche, writing and illustrating black and white series books – writing eight at a time based on a new character and situation that fitted well with the primary school curriculum. I visited a lot of schools and pretty well assumed that was me set up for life!

The internet was coming along and about to change everything. I could see it but publishers didn't believe me and I knew I had to start building an online presence. I used to be able to rely on publishers to sell enough copies to provide my income but now there are so many people taking a bite out of the cake in books that authors don't have too much left at the end.

Five years ago I innocently typed 'manga' into Google, because I kept being asked about the Japanese comic form and knew nothing about it. I came across a video by Mark Crillee and thought OMG! I could do this and show how to draw the characters from my books. The big wide world on YouTube wasn't really interested in my characters, but I did get requests to show how to draw things – I produced a couple of 'How to draw' videos and got more views in a month than I had in a year with only my characters.

It became very addictive. If you watch my early videos I sound high! People often commented on it and in fact I was high – high on a new medium and all the new skills I was learning as well as the interaction with people all around the world.

When I won the YouTube NextUp award I felt like there was nothing I couldn't do and I think I did too much. Success is a dangerous thing – it makes you want to do more and ignore the core of what works.

Since then YouTube has become integrated with Google and the rules have changed dramatically about three times. Being wedded to Google/YouTube is exhausting in that they can change things so rapidly and you have to be on your guard for the new changes, which often happen without warning. The upside is you get access to the audience that Google and YouTube provides.

I am settling at around 500,000 views per month at the moment, from a high of 750,000. The videos that inspire people to subscribe are more about technique and being an artist so now I'm moving my Drawing Channel into a more grown up, teaching art kind of channel, and starting out with a new channel called Shoobeedoodling, which will be entirely dedicated to my books, stories and characters. I have another successful channel called DrawStuffRealEasy, which has been going in different directions, but I'll focus more on showing kids how to draw in a more simple, cartoony way and build a book brand to go with it.

More importantly, I'm changing my mindset from being an author and illustrator to being an educator – this reframes the marketing approach.

Income is now earned from several sources and I've really opened my mind to the 'multiple income stream' thing. I have an app and eBooks with Apple and Amazon and it's great to see huge numbers of names putting (a little) money in my account each month. But not enough yet! I visit schools and do talks and whatever pays the bills. I know I will get the mix right in the end!

I've developed one app, mostly to prove I could do it but I've decided apps are too much work for me; they make the mind work differently – I become uncreative when programming an app as I use the logical side of my brain.

The next 12 months is all about consolidation, focus and developing markets instead of audiences. I'm planning to make 'how to draw' books and eBooks, I want to get quite a lot of my out-of-print titles available as print-on-demand and eBooks and rather than feel I have to keep coming up with new characters, I'm going to work with the ones I've already got and develop them in ways a publisher wouldn't, which is why I have got the rights back for them. I still have potentially lucrative properties that I feel have hardly been exploited at all.

I'm working on my online shop to sell digital downloads and artwork and I'm going to have a go at charging for coaching and portfolio critiques over Skype – yet another income stream! The plan is to focus my approaches to different but identified markets, have something to sell and not be afraid to make Call to Actions to buy.

My wife has allowed me to take over the front room as a studio as I'm going to film *Jackanory*-style readings of my books and there just isn't room in the shed, but the shed definitely will remain HQ as I focus and grow!"

 **www.shoorayner.com**

 **@shoorayner**

Through productising, income is being generated in boxing up your knowledge and, in the process, you are fast becoming known as an expert which means customers will be prepared to pay a margin for the actual product made by your own hands, i.e. the original item.

You become the expert and build income at the same time. What a great way to grow a business.

Go Global

Take your business to the world by taking five key steps. Harness the web to reach 1.2 billion online customers and enjoy the cultural experience that comes with trading in new territories.

In 2010, I wrote a book called *Go Global: how to take your business to the world*. Fast-forward five years and I still believe entry into new and international markets is one of the most financially rewarding and personally fulfilling ways to grow. Enabled by technology, trading via powerful marketplaces and with the quality stamp of 'Made in Britain' displayed on products and services, businesses are going global faster than ever and benefiting from the extra sales and new connections it brings.

This section offers what you need to know, with further detail and more case studies available in *Go Global* (www.enterprisenation.com/books/go-global).

These are the steps to follow:

Step 1. Research

Identify potential markets through reactive and pro-active research.

- **Reactive** – check Google Analytics (www.google.com/analytics) to see if your site is already attracting international traffic, and if selling digital products (see 'Digital products' on page 51 onwards), review your download figures on platforms such as iTunes, Amazon and GoToWebinar to identify existing demand and interest from overseas.

- **Proactive** – make the most of online resource hubs which you can find via most major high street banks, plus industry and country reports on sites including Alibaba and Open to Export. Government agency UK Trade and Investment (UKTI) has programmes to help at this stage; the Overseas Market Introduction Service (OMIS) carries out research and makes introductions on your behalf and the Export Market Research Scheme (EMRS) gives a contribution to costs towards research on new markets.

Useful links

Alibaba www.alibaba.co.uk

Open to Export www.opentoexport.com

UK Trade & Investment www.ukti.gov.uk

Export Britain www.opentoexport.com

HSBC Global Connections globalconnections.hsbc.com

Government support

Export Marketing Research Scheme (EMRS)

> 'The Export Marketing Research Scheme gives your company free, independent advice on how to carry out marketing research. It can help you decide if you should export to a new market, and advise you on how best to deliver products and services. It can also provide financial support for your marketing research project in certain circumstances.'

 www.gov.uk/export-marketing-research-scheme

Overseas Market Introduction Service (OMIS)

> 'OMIS puts you in touch directly with UKTI staff in over 100 overseas markets. It can help you access the right international contacts or partners, find the best way to do business in a market and achieve a successful market entry strategy.'

 www.gov.uk/overseas-market-introduction-service

In carrying out this research, what you're looking for is:

Country	**Customers**
Which are the countries that present the greatest opportunity? *What is the size of the target customer group and the economic/political situation?*	*How do customers in this market like to buy; what is the preferred payment method, packaging, customer support and who are their key influencers in the media and online?*
Cost	**Competition**
What is the cost of doing business in the country; getting products and services delivered, any local licenses required or sourcing agents and distributors?	*Who is the local competition and is there any potential for partnership?*

"The number of overseas shoppers browsing the web for British clothing and footwear retailers has surged in the past year. According to data from the British Retail Consortium, the Chinese were the most active, with searches on all devices from tablets to smartphones increasing by 50%, followed by Russia, France and Germany."

Kasmira Jefford, *City AM*, 28 April 2014

Step 2. Promote

With countries identified, it's time to get known. Do so by embracing social media and making friends with the bloggers, magazines and media channels with which your customers connect.

Social media

Take to Twitter, find friends on Facebook and get pinning on Pinterest to raise profile across the globe. Over one billion people are online and they're spending an increasing amount of their time on social media. Add to this the fact that 93% of shoppers make buying decisions influenced by social media, and you realise the importance of having a presence on the major platforms. Those platforms are:

- Twitter (**www.twitter.com**)
- Facebook (**www.facebook.com**)
- LinkedIn (**www.linkedin.com**)

- Pinterest (**www.pinterest.com**)
- Instagram (**www.instagram.com**)
- YouTube (**www.youtube.com**)

Consider Hootsuite (**www.hootsuite.com**) as a tool to streamline your social media activity and schedule tweets and posts to fit in with local time zones. As sales grow, consider outsourcing to a social media specialist, possibly someone based in the country, by finding talent on the marketplaces profiled on page 168.

"Having started the business with no advertising budget and promoting ourselves on Facebook, we attracted fans from all over the world and now have almost 1.5 million likes. This has translated into sales, with 75% made overseas. Morphsuits are popular the world over – in Australia, Germany, the USA – and we recently signed a deal with an Indian distributor."

FRASER SMEATON, CO-FOUNDER, MORPHSUITS

Register your site with the major search engines to increase the chances of it appearing in local results.

- Google (**www.google.com/addurl**)
- Bing (**www.bing.com/webmaster**)
- Baidu (for China) (**www.baidu.com/search/url_submit**)
- Yandex (for Russia) (**www.yandex.com**)
- The Open Directory Project (**www.dmoz.org/add.html**)

Optimise your site by having keywords you think overseas customers will be searching for and a country-specific top level domain (covered in 'Step 5: Go local' on page 105). Reach out to bloggers that appeal to your target market and offer to write guest posts and share links.

This activity and promotion costs nothing but your time and will yield results in customers finding and engaging with you online.

> *"My advice to anyone considering international trade is just be open to the opportunity and get to know the influential bloggers in that territory. Being known online is what leads to sales."*
>
> Emma Henderson, Founder, Showpony

For Kat Williams, it was her blog – and knowledge of blogging – that led her down the path of international business.

Name: Kat Williams

Business: Rock n Roll Bride

Rock n Roll Bride is a business and blog I've been following since profiling its entrepreneurial founder, Kat Williams, in 2010. Since then Kat has successfully grown the blog, gone into print and gone global.

"I was very lucky that in May 2010 my boss agreed to me going part-time. This allowed me the security of having a small income to cover the mortgage, whilst giving time to work on Rock n Roll Bride. Having the extra time to work on the blog allowed me to progress the business quickly, and in just a few months I was earning enough from it to completely supplement the income I'd earned as a full-time employee. I handed in my notice in January 2011. It was a scary time but was a step I knew I wanted – and had – to take if I wanted to really make a go of running my own business."

Kat has built the blog into one which attracts thousands of visitors eager to check out rock n roll weddings.

"In terms of growing readership, I've never really had an exponential explosion of growth. It's really just been about being consistent with what I do, posting content that people find engaging and utilising social media as much as I can."

The majority of Kat's income comes from direct advertising on the blog and a print publication that started out as a happy accident.

"I was invited to exhibit at a wedding fair. When it came to planning what to actually put on the stand I was stumped. I mean how do you really 'show' a blog? My business partner (and husband!), Gareth, came up with the idea of a brochure, showcasing some of the best blog content, to hand out to people. In the end it morphed from the initial idea of a 14-page brochure to a full 48-page beast!

When we announced on the blog we'd be handing out a free Rock n Roll Bride 'magazine' at the show people went nuts for it. People who couldn't make the show were asking where they could buy one and many people came along just so they could pick up a copy. After issue one was out of stock we decided that, clearly, this is something people wanted."

There's a blog to maintain and more magazines to produce, and what's also captured Kat's attention is a new training academy she's fast taking round the world.

"The Blogcademy is a two-day blogging workshop which I host with two US bloggers. It is an in-person workshop with 30 students (or Blogcadettes as we call them!) and we teach everything you would want to know about building and maintaining a successful blog. From writing skills to branding, photography basics to social media. as well as monetisation and how to keep motivated. We've had bloggers travel from all over the world to take part. So far we have done workshops in New York, London, Portland, Los Angeles, Australia and New Zealand. The amazing thing about the workshop is that we attract bloggers from a huge range of niches, all wanting to blog about different things. The Blogcademy isn't about creating clones of us (heaven forbid!), it's about giving our students the tools to go forth and be the very best version of themselves they can be."

Going Global is a major part of Kat's plans for growth in the next 12 months as she takes her skills of building a successful blog and shares this with people across the globe. Watch out for where this entrepreneur rocks up next!

www.theblogcademy.com

@theblogcademy

Cross border social media

Tamsin Fox-Davies is Senior Development Manager at Constant Contact and a social media pro. She offers her top tips on getting the right social media strategy when selling into new markets.

Social media is a great tool for expanding reach beyond your immediate area and the normal social media rules apply, with a couple of extra things to think about:

- In terms of which social platforms to use, ask your ideal customers which networks they use most often and start there.
- Time zones may be a factor. Make sure you post at appropriate times for where your target customers are (which might be the middle of the night for you!). Use good management tools to help with scheduling, working out the best times to post, and keeping track of who you've responded to. I like MarketMeSuite and Buffer.
- Ensure your content has enough local relevance, e.g. UK tax tips are of little use to German businesses.
- Follow local influencers in the areas where you want to work. Connect and engage with these influencers to get the attention of their followers and fans, who are likely to be (in large part) local to their home country/region.
- As always, keep things non-salesy. As an outsider you will have to work harder than a local person to build a good reputation as an interesting and helpful resource.
- Ideally tweets and posts should be in the language of the country that you are selling into, but not necessarily so. It depends on the country you're working in (some are more anglicised than others), and the industry you're part of.

If you want to sell in a country with a different language, remember that social media activity is only a small part of your customer service and acquisition. Over time, build skills and tools to deal with local customers from that country across the whole business, from marketing, to sales and customer service.

International press

Your audience is online and also reading news sites and local press. Aim for coverage via international press distribution services that offer exposure, for a fee.

- PR Newswire – sends your release to consumers, media, bloggers, investors, analysts, opinion leaders and influencers in more than 170 countries, with the option to have your news translated into over 40 languages.
  - Go Global service: www.prnewswire.com/products-services/distribute
- Business Wire – offers a US service, which reaches more than 1,000 US daily newspapers, plus radio, television and online outlets. Also offers a global service, which promotes news across international networks.
  - US service: www.businesswire.com
  - Global service: www.businesswire.com/portal/site/home/5166

"Be prepared to refashion your sales and business approach to fit the customs, approach and general dynamics of your chosen market. From a communications perspective, getting the right nuances is critical, as is positioning your product within the social vernacular. Anyone here in the UK who has cringed while watching a dubbed US commercial will know how painful it can be when these things go wrong."

GORDON TEMPEST-HAY, CEO, BLUE RUBICON

Closer to home, consider the publications that have a cosmopolitan readership. On page 165 Jane Field of Jonny's Sister tells how profile on *Country Living* magazine's Emporium page was the profile she needed for orders to start coming in from across the globe.

Campaigns and networks

Get involved with international programmes and entrepreneurial campaigns and benefit from the network of connections and resulting profile.

- Global Entrepreneurship Week (www.gew.org.uk)
- Startup Weekend (www.startupweekend.org)
- UP Global (www.up.co)

Step 3. Make sales

Make sales online or in person. The world is, quite literally, your oyster.

Online

One of the great benefits of having a website means having a window to the world; an opportunity to showcase your style, demonstrate expertise, and have browsers visit, and hopefully turn into buyers.

Template website providers such as Moonfruit (**www.moonfruit.com**) and Shopify (**www.shopify.com**) come with e-commerce built-in and, many of them, integration with inventory management and payment tools. They represent an effective route to getting online and going global as visitors experience your professional-looking online store – and click to buy in their own currency.

Payment options

Accept multiple currencies and payment types with these major payment gateways and tools:

- PayPal – easy to set up, plug PayPal into your site and sell across 193 countries and markets.
  - » **www.paypal.co.uk**
  - » **@paypaluk**
- Stripe – 'accept payments from anyone, anywhere' with this payment API built for developers and backed by the founders of PayPal. With 139 currencies included, you can charge customers at their local rate. Payments accepted online are

moved into a credit account of your choosing in 24 hours with reporting and accounting integration built-in.

» www.stripe.com

» @stripe

- Worldpay – accept credit and debit payments online, over the phone and in person with a Worldpay pay page or virtual terminal. The company supports 120 different currencies and more than 200 payment types, processing 26 million transactions every day.

  » www.worldpay.co.uk

  » @worldpay

- Sage Pay – process all types of card payments using various payment methods and across borders. This is part of accounting provider Sage, so synchs with SageOne software to keep finances in order.

  » www.sagepay.co.uk

  » @sagepay_uk

As sales grow, consider a foreign exchange account with a broker such as Caxton FX (www.caxtonfx.com) or First Rate FX (www.firstratefx.com) and keep track of currency rates and changes via XE (www.xe.com).

Add a shopping cart to an existing site and make it transactional with products such as osCommerce (www.oscommerce.com) and RomanCart (www.romancart.com).

Trading platforms

Online marketplaces have played a significant role in enabling small businesses to reach customers overseas.

For selling products, the major marketplaces you will know are:

- Etsy (www.etsy.com)
- eBay (www.ebay.co.uk)
- Amazon Marketplace (www.amazon.co.uk/sell-online)
- ASOS (www.asos.com)
- Notonthehighstreet (www.notonthehighstreet.com)

The job of these marketplaces is to attract international customers, leaving you to upload products (with professional imagery), and deliver when sales come in.

"It took about a week – my first buyer was in Hong Kong and I was so excited! In the first few months I hardly did any promotion – customers found me through Etsy. They are still finding me and 90% of my sales are to the USA, Canada and Australia. It's still a surprise to me when I receive a UK order."

Rowena Dugdale, Red Ruby Rose and Etsy seller

See page 168 for a full listing of talent marketplaces which enable graphic designers, web developers, copywriters and other professionals to get to new and international markets.

In person

Sell face-to-face by attending trade shows and events in your target territory. UK Trade and Investment (UKTI) hosts missions and offers access to trade shows for eligible businesses via two main programmes:

1. **Tradeshow Access Programme** – provides grant support for new and less experienced exporters to exhibit overseas. When applying for support from this programme, do so ahead of making travel plans and ticket purchases or your application may be rejected on the basis you are able to make the visit within your own resources and are not reliant on public support.

www.gov.uk/tradeshow-access-programme

2. **Market Visit Support** – provides guidance and funding to help companies visit a market as part of a group or delegation, hosted by an international trade advisor.

www.gov.uk/market-visit-support

For advice on whether your company can claim funds to attend missions and shows, contact an international trade advisor in your area via the UKTI website (www.ukti.gov.uk/export).

Enterprise Nation Go Global Missions

On 26 September 2014, Enterprise Nation led its first Go Global mission, taking 67 small businesses to New York. We met the city's hottest StartUps and entrepreneurs and just under half a million pounds worth of deals were done.

Based on this success, there'll be more missions in 2015 and beyond. Become an Enterprise Nation member to get all the details and Go Global with us!

Agents and Distributors

Make sales by appointing a trusted representative on the ground. An agent secures sales on your behalf and is usually paid in the form of a commission per sale. It's best to have an agreement in place so both parties have shared expectations and agreed targets from the outset.

- Guide to export agents: **www.gov.uk/export-agents**

An arrangement with a distributor involves a company or individual buying from you, and then selling on the goods or service at a higher price in their local market. This form of business may also be referred to as *wholesaling*.

Licensing

Another route to generating revenue from overseas, without having to make and ship a product, is licensing. This has worked for Alison Grieve and her invention, Safetray.

Name: Alison Grieve

Business: Safetray

"We are something of a hybrid company, having a manufacturing base in the UK to supply the majority of the world, but also having sold a license to US-based San Jamar who manufacture and distribute the Safetray product in North America.

We had known from the outset that North America would be our strongest market and had a business plan specifically for that territory. Licensing had not been part of the original plan, but when we were approached by San Jamar's parent company (after having met one of their board members at a trade show) we realised the extensive network of sales reps they already have in the territory, along with multiple distributor listings with all the key players, that it would rapidly accelerate market penetration by partnering with such a huge company.

The other attraction in licensing the IP was that a second manufacturing facility provided a reduction in risk – if there is ever an issue with one manufacturing plant, we always have another option for production.

Agreeing a license with San Jamar has added credibility to the Safetray brand not only in North America but around the world as it is a recognised brand in foodservice globally.

Licensing is an art not a science, and will vary greatly depending on the product and companies involved. We would normally expect an upfront payment to cover the income we would have expected to be making if selling in that territory ourselves, while the licensee spends some time establishing production and getting ready to launch – we might call that an exclusivity fee or a stand-still payment. We would then expect a per-unit-sold royalty with minimum guarantees for an agreed number of years. Other inclusions might be that there is a co-branding or that the tooling should be included in the sale of the licence. Some companies simply ask for an annual fee with no additional royalties. There really is no set way of negotiating a licence but I do believe it is important for a licensor to have a very clear view of what they are looking for before they commence negotiations.

We have more foodservice products in development, ready to launch in stages over the next two years. Agreeing more licenses is an important part of our strategy as it's served us well so far."

 **www.safetrayproducts.com**

 **@safetray**

Step 4: Deliver

Have products and services reach the destination on time and in budget. Sending electronic and digital files is relatively straightforward, with physical goods presenting a little more of a challenge.

Exporting brings with it a duty to inform HM Revenue & Customs in the UK, and the customs authority in the country to which parcels are being sent.

When posting packets or parcels outside of the EU, attach a CN22 (with contents up to the value of £270) or CN23 (value of over £270) declaration.

Completion will help ensure your package makes it past customs in the receiving country. There is no need for a customs declaration for packages sent within the EU.

- CN22 and CN23 declaration downloads

www.royalmail.com/business/help-and-support/I-need-advice-about-customs-requirements

Tax treatment

- **VAT** – details of exports should be included on your VAT return and if goods are leaving the European Union you don't include VAT on the invoice. Be aware of the recently introduced VAT MOSS rules when selling digital services to consumers within the EU.
- **Corporation tax** – if making sales from a UK-based business with no presence overseas, you will not be liable to pay corporation tax in the country to which you are exporting.

Handle with care

When it comes to shipping, there are a number of international courier companies from which to choose including:

- **UPS** – the largest express carrier and package delivery company in the world (**www.ups.com**)
- **DHL** – deliver to more than 120,000 destinations in 225 countries (**www.dhl.co.uk**)
- **Parcelforce Worldwide** – part of the Royal Mail Group with international shipping capability (**www.parcelforce.com**)
- **wnDirect** – the new kid on the block, enabling British e-tailers to ship effectively and expand to new locations (**www.wndirect.com**)

"As my products are small I offer free worldwide postage and charge one price for all my kits – it makes overseas buyers happy to purchase from me as they know the items will not cost them more."

Holly Hinton, Holly's Hobbies

Compare international shipping prices on price comparison platform Parcel2Go.com and get the best deal for you – and your customer.

Online satisfaction

Aim for satisfied international customers by using an online support system such as Zendesk, instant messaging via Skype, and keep updated on shared projects with overseas based partners using Basecamp and Google Docs. See page 207 for tools to deliver customer satisfaction and easy collaboration. Harnessing them will mean being on hand for customers, suppliers and partners even if your day ends when theirs begins.

Step 5: Go local

As sales expand and relations develop, consider upping investment and commitment to the market.

Start with website localisation.

- **Top level domains** – Have sub domains from your main .com site or buy a country code top-level domain (or ccTLD) such as .fr for France or .ru for Russia. This will improve search engine optimisation. Registering for some codes requires having a presence or registered company in that country, but you can check this with most major domain registration companies such as 123-reg (**www.123-reg.co.uk**) or GoDaddy (**www.godaddy.com**).
- **Hosting** – Sites hosted in the country of the user conducting the search tend to appear higher in search results so local hosting could be a consideration. Ask your domain registrar about their local hosting service provision.

"Whether you're selling car parts to Columbia, or sail-boats to Spain, proper website localisation means you have to think beyond language to the exact dialect of your target market. For example, in Spain the word for car is coche, *but in many Latin American countries* coche *is a baby-stroller. In the UK, a baby-stroller is a pram or a buggy, and if you're from Canada, a buggy is likely to be something you put your groceries in. The point is, you need to be aware of differences between dialects – this requires local linguists with local knowledge."*

Christian Arno, founder, Lingo24

- **Translation** – Whether it's just a few pages or all of them, translate your site with a free tool such as Google Translate (**translate.google.com**) or commission translation specialists such as Lingo24 (**www.lingo24.com**). Outside of your website, think about having introductory emails translated, interpreters for conference calls, and local language versions of promotional materials.
- **Imagery** – Having images on your site that resonate with an international audience will stand you in good stead to convert browsers to customers. Source relevant images from stock libraries like iStock (**www.istockphoto.com**) or search for Creative Commons licensed images you can use commercially at sites such as Compfight (**www.compfight.com**).

Having local websites, domains and translation has been a good policy for Ann-Maree Morrison as she takes her business global – and, for the first time in 11 years, outside the home.

Name: Ann-Maree Morrison

Business: Labels4Kids

After a career as an accountant and management consultant, Ann-Maree Morrison decided she wanted to do something that involved earning a living and having time to spend with the kids. Not only were her three children the motivating factor for the business, they were also the source of its idea. As her boys regularly lost their belongings, Ann-Maree decided a company producing labels for everything – rather than just clothing – would do well.

"We started the business at the beginning of 2005, selling a wide range of labels: from vinyl to stick-in and sew-on labels. It was in 2008 that orders from overseas started to come in. I wanted to see if they would increase by having the site translated into the local language. At the time, we were getting two orders per month from Germany, for example – it's now eight orders per day. Having a site in the local language made the world of difference and I haven't spent a penny on direct marketing abroad as customers find us through search engine results."

The company is now selling internationally via the UK site with dedicated sites for Germany, France, Sweden and Spain.

"We sell to the US via the UK site at the moment but Italy and Portugal and a separate US site are about to go live.

We accept payment across all the sites and in multiple currencies via Worldpay."

Since inception this international business has been based at home and round the family, but that's about to change.

"As the business grew, it became more important to have staff for translation work. We get very busy in our peak summer period and ended up having one room containing four people, another one to four people in the kitchen – and at one stage, there were even staff in the hall! My children were getting a bit frustrated with their lack of personal space and time at home and as they're getting bigger there's not really a need for me to be in the house to supervise any more.

I had been looking for a few years for a rental close to the city centre and to my home. However the cost was extortionate and as an internet business I did not really need the add-on services they offered like post franking and routing phone calls.

There was never the right office. It was either too small or too big or too far from home and in an industrial office space with hard concrete floors and no windows! I wanted something that was pleasant to work in (a bit like home).

Finally we decided it was best to buy, if we could find the right place. We did find it and moved in after nine years (and two years of pre-set up planning) in the house. It is quite daunting to have additional office costs but at least the property is owned by the business and money is not being wasted on rent."

This business, which is making sales in many corners of the globe, is run by four full-time employees including Ann-Maree plus two interns for the summer and up to three freelance translators when they're needed.

"We have ambitious plans to grow both our UK and international markets. I think we now have a really solid base for expansion with a state-of-the-art website and a new office to support the growth. We don't envisage having to grow our administration base any larger than eight staff full-time, even with more sales from more countries. The future is looking very positive."

 **www.labels4kids.com**

 **@labels4kids**

Virtual presence

Achieve a virtual presence with a:

- **Virtual PA** – or virtual assistant (VA) who operates from the country in which you wish to be represented. A VA can take calls on your behalf, routing messages back to you, as well as completing other tasks. See page 109 for details on how to find a VA, and if the US market is your target, look at Barnaby Lashbrooke's Time etc profiled on page 10. For continual call pick-up, Moneypenny (profiled on page 140) has agents in New Zealand who clock on when the UK clocks off.
- **Virtual office** – this will give you the look and feel of a local presence, without the associated costs. Display a local address

on business cards and online, without having to buy an actual office and staff it. Regus (**www.regus.com**) is the largest serviced operator in the world with 1,800 centres in 600 cities and 100 countries, meaning you can be in as many places as them!

- **Virtual number** – sign up to an international virtual number with a company like Vonage (**www.vonage.co.uk**) and not only do you get a local number to promote to clients, it also means they only pay a local rate when calling.

"The advantage is that people overseas can call you for the price of a local call if you choose a virtual number in their area code. You can have as many lines as you like and maintain a local presence anywhere you choose."

VONAGE

The virtual look and feel will take you further on this international and entrepreneurial journey but there's nothing that beats regular visits and, time permitting, learning the language and culture. It's something with which Kwintessential (**www.kwintessential.co.uk/resources/country-profiles.html**) can help and will mean you can say at the end of the day that you and your business have truly Gone Global.

Focus on What You Do Best and Outsource the Rest

Spend time on the aspect of the business you most enjoy and that makes the most of your skills and talent. Outsource and subcontract work to other experts who take on the tasks you shouldn't be doing. Here's how to go about it.

As highlighted throughout this book, many modern businesses are focused on growing turnover and profitability as opposed to headcount. This is for a number of reasons:

- Business owners don't want to take on the legalities and expense that comes with employing people full-time – and then managing and motivating them full-time.
- Having started a business at home and enjoyed the 60-second commute and running the business around the family, it's hard to move out. Recruiting people means having to do that – or moving them in!
- Top professionals and experts are 'going portfolio', meaning quality talent is available on a freelance basis, and there are a number of websites on which you can find this talent

It's for these reasons that the majority of Enterprise Nation members are looking to grow the business by focusing on what they do best and outsourcing the rest.

"Successful people are good at determining where their strengths and weaknesses lie and then outsourcing accordingly"

Rob Welch, Founder, smallcarBIGcity

You can do this by following a two-step process:

1. Focus on what you do best – involves deciding on what you do best
2. Outsource the rest – involves finding the talent to fill the gaps

Focus on what you do best

If there was a recipe for successfully growing a business, it would involve three key ingredients:

1. Taking care of customers
2. Attracting new customers
3. Keeping on top of finances and cash flow

These are the three fundamentals that should be given attention for a business to thrive. As a business owner, you will know there are many functions beneath each one!

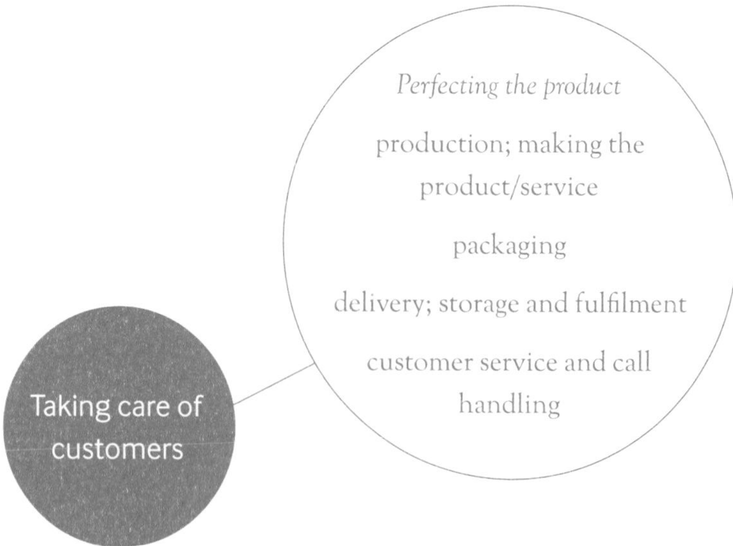

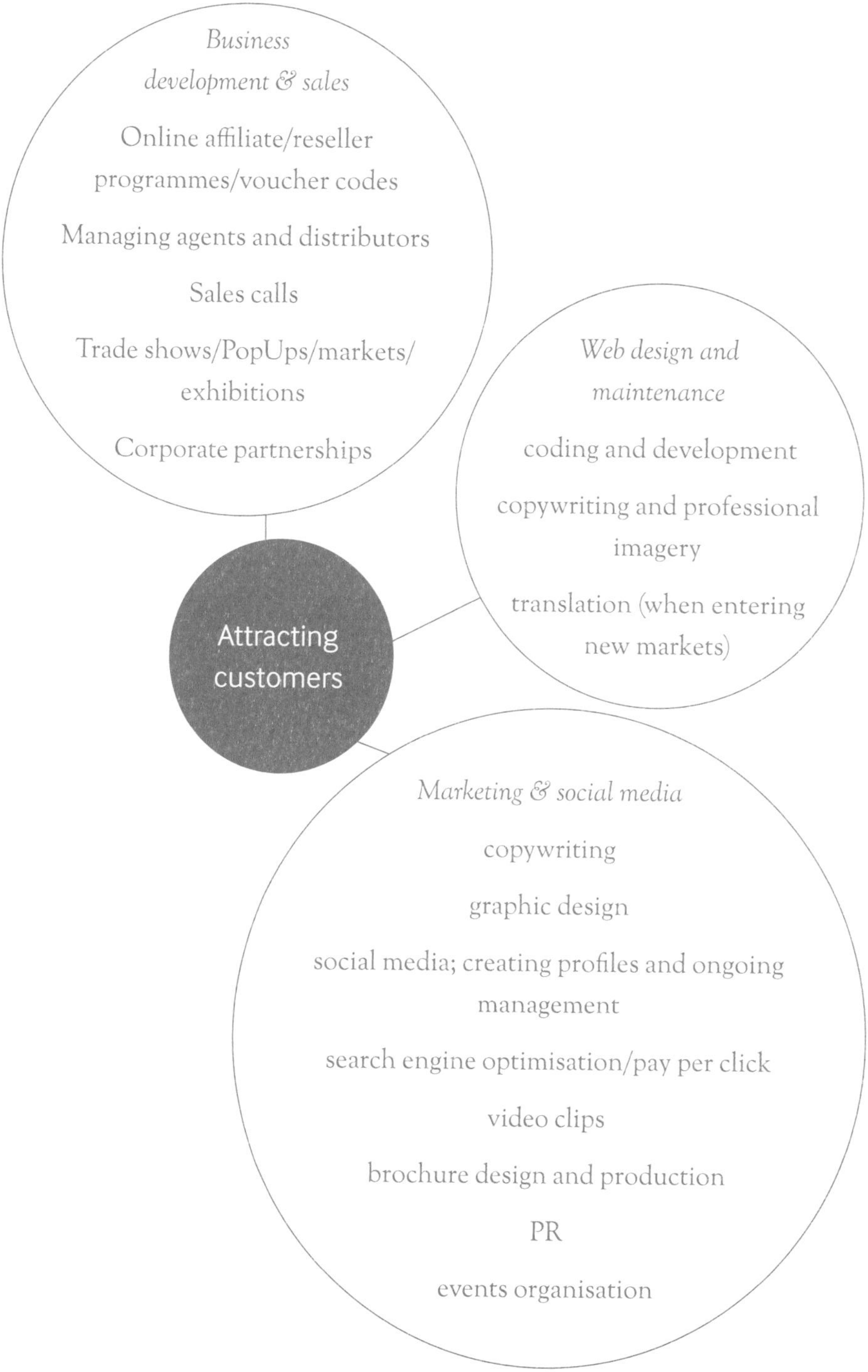

Business development & sales
Online affiliate/reseller programmes/voucher codes
Managing agents and distributors
Sales calls
Trade shows/PopUps/markets/ exhibitions
Corporate partnerships
Attracting customers
Web design and maintenance
coding and development
copywriting and professional imagery
translation (when entering new markets)
Marketing & social media
copywriting
graphic design
social media; creating profiles and ongoing management
search engine optimisation/pay per click
video clips
brochure design and production
PR
events organisation

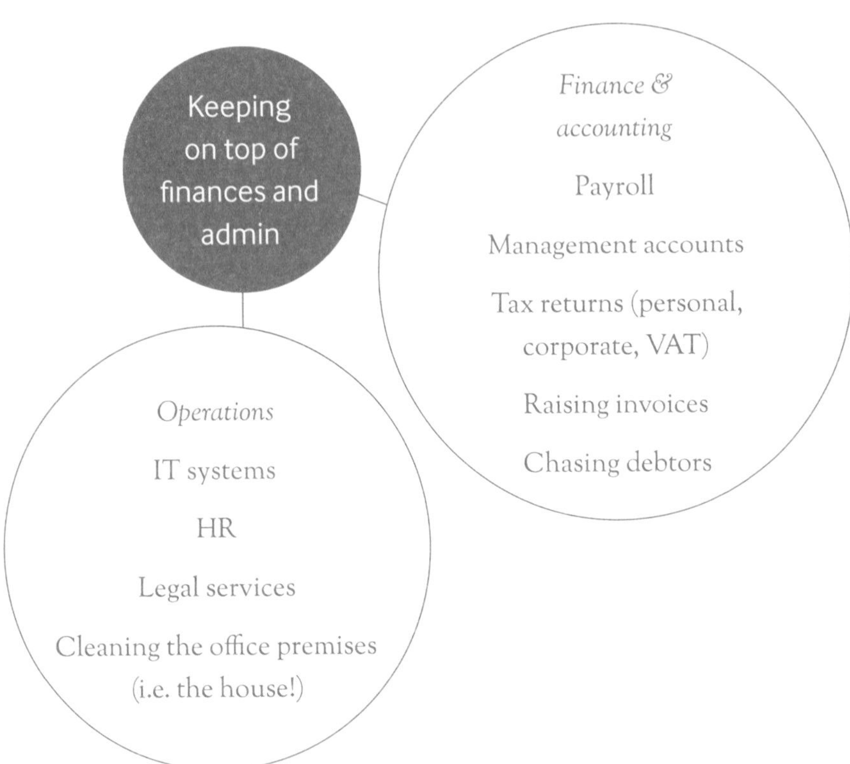

Go through the list and choose the elements at which you excel. With that decided, you want to become the best you can be at this particular skill and be known as such. For Alison Battisby, the skill at which she most excelled was social media and it is this skill that she's turned into a full-time business.

Name: Alison Battisby

Business: Avocado Social

It was during her postgraduate diploma in journalism that Twitter came to Alison's attention as a useful tool to promote her own talents and brand.

"I saw an opportunity to use it as a way to promote my services as a journalist and blogger, make contacts and find news stories. It was exciting to be using a new tool and colleagues began to come to me for advice. I really enjoyed showing others how to use it and explaining the benefits of social media and that's when I realised I should continue doing it – for businesses."

Alison's approach has been to focus on her own area of expertise and recommend trusted contacts to clients who are after other types of online work such as website design, pay per click (PPC) and search engine optimisation (SEO).

"Word of mouth and networking drives so much of my new business and that means having a good reputation is key. I make sure I touch base with my contacts and make the effort to see them every few months. This way they are more likely to recommend me when they hear someone needs social media help, as I am the first person that springs to mind. I am also a keen blogger, and tend to offer free posts to a number of well-read blogs, as long as I know they will promote it in their emails and on their social media channels. Obviously keeping my own social media and blog up to date also helps!"

 **www.alisonbattisby.co.uk**

 **@alisonbattisby**

Time is money

Across all these functions, consider one thing:

> How much of your time would it take to do the task versus the cost of outsourcing it?

For example, say you are running a cake-making business and at the moment you're doing everything as there's only enough money in the pot to support you. You are:

- Making the cakes
- Packaging the cakes
- Attending shows to make sales
- Maintaining the website
- Promoting the business through social media
- Responding to customer enquiries
- Posting and packaging cakes
- Attending promotional events and doing interviews with local media
- Running the accounts

That's a lot of tasks! Say you've been through the above exercise and decided that what you do best of all is sales and business development. You enjoy meeting customers at trade shows and farmers' markets and customers like to buy from you as the business owner. You have aspirations to pitch to a large retailer and then there's that plan to sell wholesale to local restaurants and delis... if only you had the time. Sound familiar?

Outsourcing production, packaging and posting is a big step but what it could do is:

- Earn you five more hours per day to focus on sales; that's 25 hours per week (based on a 5-day working week which is the minimum for most small business owners!)
- With that extra time, you make 20 more sales of a £25 cake which is equal to an extra £500 per week in the business, i.e. £26,000 per year
- This is the budget from which funding comes to outsource to a third party

Whether you're making cakes or writing creative strategies, the same applies. Spending more time on the aspect of the business at which you excel will bring in income for you to outsource the elements you don't enjoy so much, to people who do.

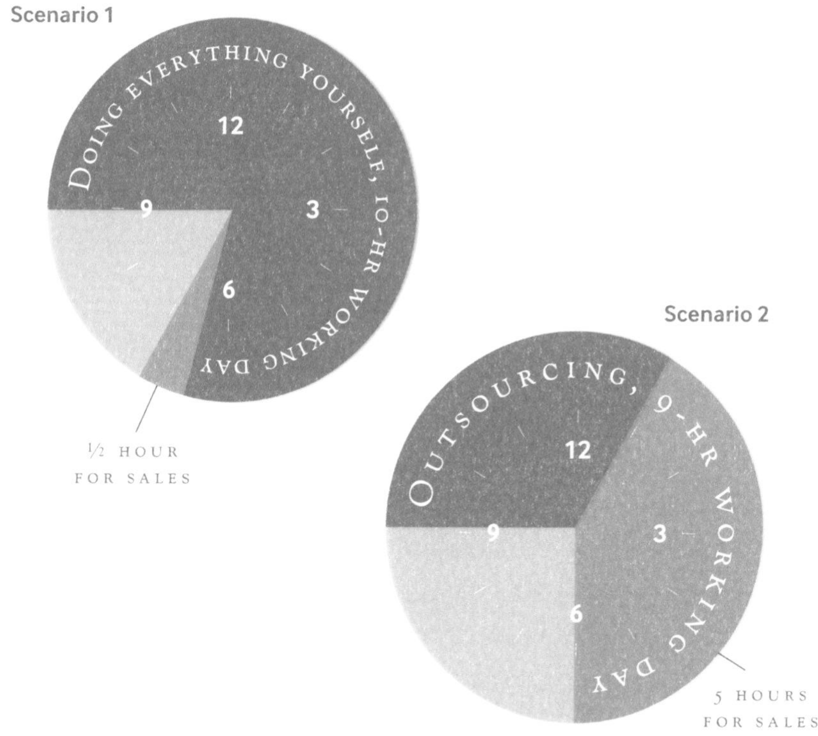

When starting out I recommend you spend time working on all tasks as you want to get a good grounding in all areas of your business. If you have done the task yourself, you'll be better briefed when it comes to finding the ideal partner to take it on. For example, if you're outsourcing social media, having done it yourself for the first six to 12 months, you'll know the kind of tone that fits the brand and the type of messages and campaigns to which your fans and followers respond. Learn the ropes yourself before handing them on to others.

Outsource the rest

Running a virtual team means you get all the good bits of a working relationship. Also, since you don't need to share a physical workspace, you can look for workers from further afield, which can save you money and widen the talent pool.

When it comes to outsourcing functions and tasks, here are the main ones to consider and places to look for the perfect partner.

Production

Customers are after a well-made product that meets (if not surpasses) their expectations and arrives on time in good condition. If you're busy out and about making sales, it could soon be the case that you need to outsource production to others.

Over the past four to five years I've seen significant growth in the number of people turning a hobby or talent into a business. This has led to a flourishing artisan and handmade market. This section is for those businesses: companies selling a tangible product that needs to be made using craftsmanship and labour.

If you have a business selling professional services or technical products that are transmitted, 'Top 10 sites on which to find the talent you're after' on page 168 shows you the platforms on which you will find talented individuals to which you can outsource production of anything from apps to eBooks.

For product-based businesses, here are your options:

Community outsourcing

One of the finest examples of this I've seen is US-based Alabama Chanin, founded by fashion entrepreneur Natalie Chanin in Florence, Alabama. Natalie spoke at the 2012 Hello Etsy event about how she has grown the business through outsourcing production to neighbours and skilled local artisans:

On securing a large contract: "I ran an ad saying part-time sewing and quilting skills required and some of the ladies are still sewing with us today; a decade later. We went from a t-shirt company to a full collection company. Now we have seven of us in the office and 35 to 50 working in the field at any given time."

On the relationship with this workforce of artisans: "I act as an agent for them. I am the designer and owner of the company but I take their work out into the world and make it possible for stores like Barneys to see the work they are doing."

On how this arrangement works financially: "We send out a bid sheet. Our artisans bid for the pieces, complete the work, and we then sell them."

On expanding the brand and styles to customers who could not afford original pieces: "I was approached to write a book and said yes as I wanted to show that if you can't afford to buy it, you can afford to make it yourself or have someone in your community do it. A whole new appreciation came about for our collection as people could understand the time it takes to make a piece, but we now sell materials and supplies to anyone who wants to do it themselves, from our store."

Listen to the full talk and presentation here: www.livestream.com/etsy/video?clipId=pla_bee90884-dd7e-45c0-85e5-bfc6b0139a43

Suzi Warren decided to outsource her production to workshops and printers across the UK.

Name: Suzi Warren

Business: Twisted Twee

Having worked as an art director in advertising for 15 years, Suzi Warren started Twisted Twee in September 2003, a year after her daughter was born. When Suzi started, she was hands-on in delivering everything the business required.

"I started by doing all the design and production myself. I still do all the designing as that is the bit I love to do but I also hand-printed every t-shirt as I was too risk averse to buy for bulk printing."

Suzi now outsources to three silkscreen printers in the UK to print her t-shirts, pillowcases and tea towels.

"I found the first one about a week after I started – by literally trawling the internet. They are the only printers in the UK to use organic ink. I still use them for all my t-shirts. The other two I came across after recommendations by other designer-makers and have been working with them both for about five years. I have a couple of back-up printers as well, in case any of the first ones are too busy to fulfil a quick turnaround. The garments themselves I have made in France and the UK."

The secret to success in these relationships is, says Suzi, "Paying on time and being clear about exactly who is responsible for quality control".

Suzi sells her products via stockists all over the world. These were found in the early days by exhibiting at trade shows such as Top Drawer and sending free samples to shops Suzi wanted to be seen in, but she is now on the receiving end of enquiries.

"Shops find me and orders are just taken over email. I'm rather ashamed to say I rarely meet the owners of the shops I sell to. I simply send out an email with new products every few months and shops top up with what they'd like. It's incredibly easy really and very time efficient."

As with every business owner, time is the most precious asset and Suzi is assisted in growing the business by a team who help this entrepreneur dedicate her time to focusing on what she does best.

"I have a very loyal team of Twees. Fellow mums who I have known for ages that have worked with me for about six years now. They are permanent part-timers, usually working three days a week during school hours. They deal with customer queries, print and post the personalised items, keep track of the websites we sell through and forward the bulk of the orders to the warehouse who ship the goods out. The warehouse is not my own but a fulfilment company that packs and posts for a number of small businesses called The Fulfillment Company (**www.thefulfillmentco.com**). I started using them about five years into my business when I could no longer cope with storing all the stock in my garage! They have been superb and are fantastically efficient. All of this means my time is spent on designing new products which is what I started this business to do."

 **www.twistedtwee.co.uk**

Made in Britain

For companies that do have physical product as their livelihood, there is increasing appetite to have the tag 'Made in Britain' as this carries with it great provenance and sales potential abroad. 'UK products are on the rise, with 'Made in Britain' a badge of quality that draws the eye of wealthy consumers in emerging markets' reported the *Financial Times* in 2013 (**www.ft.com/cms/s/0/841a2a16-df44-11e2-a9f4-00144feab7de.html**).

This is something footwear entrepreneur Janan Leo knows all about. Hers is a business we have followed throughout our books; Janan was in *Working 5 to 9* as she started her business alongside a day job, in *Go Global* as she outsourced production to Asia and sold her collection of stylish pumps all over the world, and her story continues here as she looks to bring manufacturing back to Britain and increases growth through effective outsourcing.

Name: Janan Leo

Business: CocoRose London

In powering the growth of their company selling foldable ballet pumps, Janan and her business partner, Gareth, outsource many areas of the business from manufacturing to PR, and graphic design to fulfilment, so most of their time can be directed at managing and working with select partners. This list of partners recently expanded with the addition of a UK manufacturer who is producing a new and luxury collection. Finding this particular supplier took time and dedication.

"In my mind the 'find a supplier challenge' is made up of two parts; firstly, I think it has a lot to do with scale and how businesses wanting to make products in the UK can realistically scale up, therefore making it worthwhile for suppliers to work with them, i.e. appetite from the manufacturers to take on small volume orders. Secondly, as ever in retail, there is the challenge of price and being able to increase your price to reflect the cost of British production and still be sure of making sales."

In addressing these two points, Janan decided she did want to scale up her business and could feasibly launch a luxury collection that would have the stamp 'Made in Britain' and so sell for a higher sum.

"Having made the decision to go ahead, finding suppliers came down to a case of driving the project and physically getting out there and chatting with as many suppliers/

bodies as possible to create a list of graded suppliers. This is something that government should definitely be able to help with, if they're up for the challenge!"

Janan is following the principles in this book and looking to sell the product that comes off the production line by outsourcing.

"Most of our sales activity is outsourced, using agents and distributors for particular territories. As a growing business, we dedicate a lot of our time to managing cash flow and future funding needs. There are certain areas which we would never outsource such as design and development of our new collections, which is the heart of the brand."

In selecting their partners, Janan and Gareth tend to rely on recommendation and word of mouth.

"Finding our manufacturing partners has largely been through painstaking research followed by getting on a plane or, in the case of our Luxury Heritage Made in England range, getting in the car, and heading out to visit factories. PR has predominantly been through recommendations and in the case of our sales agents and distributors, the majority of our relationships have formed at or following trade shows, or having our products seen in a particular boutique."

The two founders have cultivated strong relationships with suppliers. So much so that this close-knit team feel as if they are part of the same company, which is an advantage as everyone is motivated to work towards common goals.

"This takes a lot of hard work on both sides and is supported with shared plans, whether marketing, sales or operations. Reporting is essential, whether this be quarterly with distributors, monthly with sales agents during the season or daily with our supply chain partners. To manage the everyday running of the business, calls and email are key and Skype has been such a great development as it lets us chat easily with partners overseas, which is a huge advantage. We try and meet with our partners as much as possible, as we believe in the good old-fashioned way of connecting with people. Finally, I don't know where we'd be without our Blackberrys!"

Four years in and Janan has taken the decision to hire staff and increase the size of the team. She is fully aware this will cost in the form of salary, National Insurance contributions and other expenses as well as taking time to find the right fit.

"A great solution for small businesses looking to take on staff, and what has helped us bridge the gap, has been the opportunity to recruit interns for a specific period of time, with the view to taking them on full-time if the agreement is mutual."

Whoever is chosen will do well in this company which continues to house ambitious growth plans.

"This year is an exciting one for us as it sees us open the first two standalone Cocorose London boutiques, in Europe and Asia, so our focus will be on the stores as well as growing the range of Luxury Heritage Made in England shoes, working with the factory and distributors to export the collection whilst continuing to innovate and lead our niche market of foldable ballet pumps."

Entrepreneurial people – please apply!

 **www.cocoroselondon.com**

 **@cocoroselondon**

Finding a supplier

Recognising the issues faced by entrepreneurs in sourcing manufacturers, Kate Hills, founder of Make it British (**www.makeitbritish.co.uk**) has launched a 'Find a Manufacturer' service for any company looking to keep production in Britain. Enquiries to the service are up 220% compared with the previous 12 months. I asked Kate how the service works.

How do you identify the manufacturers on your directory and are they willing/able to deliver small volume orders?

The manufacturers in the directory have been identified through a number of different sources. Some have been through word of mouth – I always ask companies with great quality product where it has been made – and others from manufacturers contacting me telling me about their services. I try and personally get out to as many manufacturers as possible (I recently covered 12 factories in two days in Leicester), but this is not always possible.

I have a series of questions that I ask each one in order to identify which type of client they would be most suitable for. One of these is 'what is your minimum order quantity and do you work with start-up businesses?' I find many of them will actually consider small orders, but there are various caveats to it. For instance, they will often ask for samples to be paid for upfront, at double the production cost at least. They will also ask new businesses to make a payment before they start production for them.

Sadly, start-ups have got a bad reputation with many manufacturers. This is due to a number of factors: not having realistic expectations about what can be achieved and in what timescale, not sticking to timescales and deadlines, and not having enough financial resource behind them to keep production flowing as it needs to.

Are you seeing an increase in enquiries from companies wanting to keep production in Britain? If so, what are the most popular categories?

Most definitely. Requests for our find-a-manufacturer service are 220% up on this time last year. The most popular category is clothing and leather goods, but I think that is more down to how we rank in Google for terms relating to this, rather than category demand. We're just about to launch a dedicated platform for people that want to find and work with UK clothing and textile manufacturers. Not only will there be an online directory of all of my manufacturer contacts, but also advice on how to get the best from working with these manufacturers – from both the designer and factory owner's point of view.

How do you match the small business owner to the manufacturer? Is it based on sector/geography/volume of order?

At the moment it is completely tailored to each individual's requirements. Ideally I would recommend factories on the doorstep of the small business, but specialists are often based in certain areas of the country, for instance many of the best leather goods manufacturers are in Walsall. Designers need to realise they will have to travel to visit their manufacturer – but it is still much better than going to China!

I always recommend people visit the factories to get the best out of them and really understand what they are capable of. Factory owners rarely answer emails and you can't beat meeting people face-to-face in order to spark up a good rapport. It can be the difference between a factory taking on your business or not, particularly if you are a young business.

Do you think we will continue to see production come back to Britain and will it become more economic to do so?

Most definitely. When you know the big retailers are also bringing their production back to the UK you know there is a financial advantage to it. There is now less disparity between the cost of offshore and local manufacturing, and when you factor in shorter lead times, lower shipping costs and the value that the 'Made in Britain' label adds to your product, it is definitely worth using UK manufacturers. We are taking Make it British offline in the form of 'Meet the Manufacturer' events that will enable designers and manufacturers to network together and help manufacturers show what they are capable of. So many of them don't leave their factories from one week to the next – it's time to let everyone know they exist!

 **www.makeitbritish.co.uk**

 **@makeitbritish**

Elizabeth Carrick knew from the outset she wanted to keep production in Britain and put in the hours to find the perfect partner.

Name: Elizabeth Carrick

Business: Blonde + Ginger

Having worked with manufacturers from all over the world in her previous career as a senior fashion buyer for Debenhams and the Shop Direct group, Liz Carrick knew the pros and cons of working with manufacturers in the UK.

"Whilst manufacturing in Britain is more costly than overseas, I wanted Blonde + Ginger to be a limited edition fashion label and not mass-produced. Factories abroad are set up for much bigger volumes – hence the pricing is cheaper. I did not want to produce hundreds of the same item – there is enough mass-produced fashion on the high street already. I knew I wanted to appeal to a fashion customer that wanted something unique; a customer who wants high quality contemporary clothing, without having to pay high-end designer prices."

With this vision clearly in mind, Liz started the process of looking for a UK production partner.

"I did lots of research, had many meetings and spent hours travelling the length and breadth of the country to find the manufacturer I felt was right for producing my label. It was important to me that I found someone who loved the designs and fully understood what I needed to achieve in the finish, fit and mak- up. In the first collection I used a lot of leather which is something many manufacturers cannot touch due to the machinery needed to sew it, so this limited my options. Cost was also key as I found many fantastic manufacturers operating in and around London but most were just too costly for my business plan. I finally found a partner in Wales and we've been working well together ever since."

As well as being able to promote her line as Made in Britain and not mass-produced, Liz also benefits from working to quicker lead times and being able to fully oversee the process – from sampling to production – more easily than if the garments were being produced overseas. Liz and the manufacturer are in regular contact by phone, email and visits.

"Building a strong working relationship and having constant communication has enabled both sides to feel happy with how we are progressing. I also feel my manufacturer understands my 'design eye' and what I want to achieve with the product so this saves a lot of time when it comes to discussing new patterns and design specs. I personally feel it's important to have regular face-to-face meetings as at the end of the day this is your label and it's your responsibility to make sure the product is how you intend it to be from start to finish."

Over the next 12 months Liz is progressing talks with stores and boutiques to carry the label, so is focused on finding the right stockists as well as developing new collections.

"I have had such a great response from stores and customers to the label being 'Made in Britain' as people are more aware and conscious of what they buy and where it is produced. It's not just about finding the cheapest clothing anymore –

investment fashion is on the increase as the consumer wants their wardrobe to be more versatile and last longer than one season. I intend to keep Blonde + Ginger produced in Britain as this is an important feature of my label and I really want to see manufacturing thrive again in this country as we have such a fantastic reputation for it!"

 **www.blondeandginger.com**

 **@blondegingeruk**

"At King of Shaves we own the product IP (whether that is the design, formulation, patenting, IP protection, trademarking or application of know-how) and then work with the world's best manufacturers in making that product, then assume responsibility for marketing it. Where possible, we work with British designers and manufacturers; however, in the 'cutting edge' sector we operate in, this is not always possible, so we do have co-development and co-manufacturing partnerships, the largest of which is with Kai Group of Japan."

Will King, Founder, King of Shaves

Makers on the Move

As the number of designer/makers is on the increase, so are the facilities available to them. Witness the rise of 3D printing and workshop spaces such as Makerversity (**www.makerversity.org**) and Fab Lab (**manchesterfablab.manufacturinginstitute.co.uk**) where you can carry out DIY production.

Global manufacturing

It may be that the economics of UK manufacturing don't suit your business model so you have to look further afield. This is where China's largest trading website, Alibaba.com, plays a role as it connects you with thousands of manufacturers and suppliers from across Asia.

Molly Morgan is the company's European head of PR and says:

> "The secret to success is to be specific about delivery timescales and expectations; agree shipping arrangements and cost in writing before completing any transaction and take advantage of services such as AliSourcePro which is a customised service that allows a qualified list of suppliers to bid for your business, based on your requirements. You quickly receive qualified leads that are easy to compare in a single dashboard. Alibaba.com's forums have been set up so you can ask questions and share knowledge. The 'Ask an Expert' feature gives buyers and suppliers regular advice on everything from shipping to legal questions."

It was a website and forum that came in handy when mum of two and Gear to Go founder Kate Castle went camping and came up with her idea for a lightweight portable toilet, Boginabag.

> "Since launching my first product, Boginabag, I've also introduced a foldable water bottle and an off-road cool bag with all items

sourced from China and factories found on Alibaba. I would love to produce in the UK but because of the type of products I sell it doesn't seem possible to find factories producing what I need. The business is growing and we moved out of my home at the start of 2013. We had outgrown the home office and I wanted to take on an additional member of staff. She's a business administration apprentice which means her salary is assisted by a government grant. Together, we're in talks with various international distributors having now established ourselves in Germany and Australia and there are two new products we hope to introduce to the UK market. None of this would be possible without an effective route to outsource manufacturing to China."

Consider approaching trade bodies to ask for help in securing a production partner as they often know the manufacturers that specialise in your sector and are prepared to take on order volumes to suit your size.

Trade bodies to source manufacturing partners include:

BODY	
British Footwear Association	www.britishfootwearassociation.co.uk
UK Fashion & Textile Association	www.ukft.org
British Furniture Manufacturers	www.bfm.org.uk
Food & Drink Federation	www.fdf.org.uk
Manufacturing Advisory Service	www.mymas.org

Crafts Council	www.craftscouncil.org.uk
Cosmetic, Toiletry & Perfumery Association	www.ctpa.org.uk

Production partners

Big businesses are seeing the virtue in making their assets and infrastructure available to small ones; and this includes help when it comes to production. Sheffield-based manufacturing company Gripple has created Incub (www.incub.co.uk, @incub_ideas) to help anyone with a good idea get their product to market, at speed. Gripple offers the weight of its manufacturing capability as well as skills in HR, marketing, financial management, etc. so you essentially outsource the bulk of the business to an experienced company who shows you the ropes.

Similarly, northeast-based JML (www.jmlinventors.com), which has a successful track record of selling household and consumer goods in 80+ markets, is now in the business of hosting pitch days for inventors with an idea who are happy to outsource production and market development to experts in the company. PR man Jonathan O'Connor says of the exercise: "JML will work with the inventor to take the product to market. It would initially go through a trial process (trialling in 40 stores) and then if it succeeds in this phase, we would roll it out nationally in the UK and then across the globe." Not a bad outsourcing deal at all!

See the Accelerate section for more opportunities to expedite your route to market with big business as a partner.

Delivery, storage and fulfilment

Attending a talk from Johnny Earle, founder of the successful and eponymous brand Johnny Cupcakes (www.johnnycupcakes.com), you hear the story of how in the early days he stored t-shirts in his parents' attic from where he would package orders and post them across the United States. He soon started receiving letters from customers:

'My t-shirt arrived and it smelt of cigarettes'

'My t-shirt arrived and it was covered in cat hair'

You get the message. Johnny was smoking in that attic with his cat as company. Good for Johnny, not so good for the customers. It was then he realised he needed to outsource fulfilment. Also known as 'pick and pack', this is the process by which someone else stores your product and, when an order comes in, they are the one to pick the product, pack it, and ship to the customer. No smoking and no cats. At least not on the inside of the building!

Companies that provide this kind of service include MyWarehouse and Amazon.

MyWarehouse

MyWarehouse enables any online retailer, whether you're receiving one or hundreds of orders, to outsource fulfilment on a pay-as-you-go pricing basis. There are no set-up or monthly fees or minimum contract periods. You simply pay for what gets done and can start and finish the service to suit you.

The company has recently expanded its offering to add MyMessage and MyWrap so you can personalise products too. Founder of MyWarehouse, Andy Reedman, answered some questions on what the service offers and how it helps business owners focus on what they do best.

Where is your fulfilment centre?

Milton Keynes.

Does the small business owner send product to you or can they arrange for their manufacturer to send direct to you? i.e. it could be the small business owner never touches the product

Typically, most sellers simply give our address to their supplier. About 90% of our clients never meet us so yes, they never touch the product once they have successfully sourced a good manufacturer.

Can small businesses have product delivered in boxes with their own company branding?

Yes. We offer a service called 'myWrap' specifically for clients that want to use their own boxes, or have their products wrapped in tissue paper, have free gifts added, etc. One client asked us to spray perfume in the box just before sealing!

How do you charge and what are the rates?

Start-ups and small businesses account for every penny they spend and hate surprises so we have a simple price list. We invoice monthly and include detailed spreadsheets itemising costs so the customer knows exactly where the costs have been incurred. Pick and pack starts at £1.49 per item, storage at 40p per cubic foot per month, packaging from 30p per item and courier for next-day delivery is £6.49 per item.

There are no monthly contracts or set-up fees. What we offer is a pay-as-you-go order fulfilment service for online retailers. This also means businesses can choose to stay with us for as long or as little as they like. We have some clients who just use us in peak seasons such as Christmas.

Can you help a small business that sells multiple products?

Yes, a single company could have up to 2,000 products! You simply upload the products to a secure online management system via a spreadsheet, or if you use a shopping cart or template website such as Magento or Shopify or you're selling via a marketplace such as eBay or Amazon, we can retrieve this data on your behalf. What we require are the dimensions and weight of the products so we can plan storage and pick/pack. Each product also has to have a barcode so it can be tracked by our staff in the fulfilment centre.

Have you seen an increase in the amount of custom from small business?

Yes. As a business it took us a bit of time to work out that our best clients were online sellers producing less than 1000 orders a month. This is because our service is perfect for them, whereas sellers producing more orders will be attractive to more fulfilment companies. At the moment, there are very few fulfilment companies that will deal with start-ups and small businesses because other fulfilment houses require volume to achieve economies of scale. We had to develop our own system complete with bespoke IT to enable us to operate in a way that we don't mind if a client generates one order a month or 100 a day.

What are the most common products you pick and pack?

T-shirts, toys, books, babycare, clothing, shoes, stationery, perfume, gadgets, beer. As long as the product is less than 1.5m in length, is not hazardous or illegal, to us it is a product with a barcode on it which we can store, pick and deliver.

Can the small business owner track inventory?

Yes. They can interrogate their data in many ways, from stock reports and returns as well as reports to help them sell better, such as seeing which customer bought which product.

Can the customer track the delivery?

Yes. Our whole system is available free of charge to clients. This means they can integrate the MyWarehouse system into the back-end of their own website (including template sites such as Shopify, Magento, POWA, etc.) so relevant data can be displayed to their own customers. Apart from saving our clients time in tracking down their data, it also reduces their own customer service issues by giving customers the information they need on the website. This also applies to orders taken from Amazon, eBay, Play and other channels.

Can you ship outside the UK?

Yes. Our buying power means clients can save money when shipping abroad, e.g. Next-day delivery to the United States from only £12.99.

What's the smallest level of orders with which you deal?

There is no minimum because we operate at maximum efficiency all the time, meaning we can manage one order a month or 100 orders a day.

Amazon

With Fulfilment by Amazon (FBA) you store your products in Amazon's fulfilment centres, and Amazon packs and ships as well as providing customer service for the products. There is a clear run-through of how it works on the website (services.amazon.co.uk/services/fulfilment-by-amazon/how-it-works.html).

Essentially you send your products to Amazon and upload a listing of products to Amazon's system. On receipt, Amazon scans your products so you can virtually monitor inventory. When a customer order comes in, Amazon picks and ships the product and provides tracking for the customer. This is a service for products you sell via Amazon, via third-party marketplaces, or your own website.

It's reliable but one critique I've heard is you cannot send products in your own branded boxes as all orders go out in Amazon-branded packaging.

In terms of costs, you pay a storage fee based on the volume of product in the fulfilment centre, a pick and pack fee depending on dimensions and weight and whether the product category is media or non-media, and a fee to cover shipping charges. Details on pricing can be found here: **services.amazon.co.uk/services/fulfilment-by-amazon/pricing.html**

There is no minimum order so regardless of your volume, any business can outsource fulfilment to Amazon.

The company has more than 20 fulfilment centres in Europe, meaning this is a service that will scale well with international expansion (covered in the Go Global section).

If you don't currently sell on Amazon, you sign up for a Merchant Account, integrating Fulfillment by Amazon during the registration process. If you are already selling on Amazon, you simply add Fulfilment by Amazon to your account.

In a *Fast Company* article, Amazon founder, Jeff Bezos, outlined the benefits to small business:

"Sellers are highly incentivized to use Fulfillment by Amazon (known as FBA). Rather than shipping their products themselves after a sale is made on the Amazon site, these retailers let Amazon do the heavy lifting, picking and packing. Sellers get access to Prime shipping speeds which can help them win new customers and can allow them to sell at slightly higher prices."

SOURCE: **www.fastcompany.com/3014817/amazon-jeff-bezos**

In-house fulfilment

Adam Taylor co-founded PetShopBowl in 2001 as an online store selling pet food and accessories. The company managed to secure a top deal on space and fulfilment which came about by chance.

"We stumbled on the healthcare and beauty distribution business, DCS Europe, when we were interviewed for a newspaper article. We then contacted DCS for advice and after a first meeting were offered warehouse space and other resources in exchange for setting up an e-commerce website for them. It was a great example of a small company working with a big one in a perfect exchange of skills for physical resources. It really helped our business get off to the right start."

Customer service and call handling

Having delivered a quality product to your customer, they may have questions on anything from usage to returns. Outsource this function to professionals or even to your customers!

Moneypenny

This company is the outsourced partner of choice for thousands of small business owners who want calls answered in a professional manner at all times. After opening an account, you are allocated a Moneypenny PA who picks up the phone using your company name and, based on your preferences, either routes the call to your phone or takes a message and sends a text so you can respond in your own time. You can set preferences each day and keep in touch with your Moneypenny PA via phone, email, Twitter, Moneypenny online or an app. After a free trial there is a three-month minimum contract and thereafter one month's notice to close the account. With Moneypenny having recently opened in New Zealand, they can now also offer round-the-clock support!

"For small businesses the cost of employing someone to answer the phone is usually prohibitive and yet the value of a single call can be huge. What price can you place on a missed call from your most important client or a new prospect? It's about taking control and knowing you can spend time in your meeting or with your head down writing a proposal without having to be disturbed. The main drivers for most clients are to make themselves look bigger and more professional and to grow their business by capturing every single call and new opportunity."

Joanna Swash, Marketing Director, Moneypenny

Virtual PAs

On page 109 we look at outsourcing your admin duties to virtual PAs who could also be on call to receive your calls and respond to customers.

Get Satisfaction

Have customers deliver support for you with software that enables customers to get answers to their online questions through searching answers already provided by others. According to the company, 'Get Satisfaction powers 70,000 active customer communities hosting more than 35 million consumers each month'. The website hosts a resource centre with all you need to know about creating customer support communities (**getsatisfaction.com/corp/resource-center**).

The small business option is $425 per month, so a pricey piece of software but, again, calculate the time it will save you and potentially the extra custom it will bring in the form of happy customers.

Zendesk

Customers email you via Zendesk support which automatically creates a ticket to which you respond. The tool, created in Denmark and now located in the US, serves a worldwide market of 30,000 customers. It's the tool we use at Enterprise Nation. It's easy to use and cost-effective too.

 **www.zendesk.com**

 **@zendesk**

Accounting

One of the top items that should be on your 'Things to Outsource' list is accounting. That's because accounting not only requires a specific skill, it also requires up-to-date knowledge on all the changes underway with VAT thresholds, real-time reporting, tax brackets and payroll penalties. You can choose to become a qualified accountant yourself but I suggest you go look for one who can take this on for you!

KPMG is one of the biggest names in accounting and they recently launched a dedicated accounting service for small and growing businesses, which makes up part of the Enterprise Nation member package of benefits. Outsourcing accounts to them offers peace of mind and managed cash flow.

"Tell your accountant what you're planning to do and check whether they offer the services you will need to build your business. Tell them the accounting records you keep and ask if they can suggest improvements. Ask after fee levels and who will do the work. These are some of the questions to ask to determine if an accountant is right for you and your business."

Clive Lewis, Head of Enterprise at the Institute of Chartered Accountants

Useful Links

- Institute of Chartered Accountants in England and Wales, Business Advice Service: **find.icaew.com/pages/bas**, **@icaew_bas**
- KPMG Small Business Accounting: **www.kpmgenterprise.co.uk**
- Enterprise Nation Marketplace – home to hundreds of accountants on hand to offer help with compliance and/or access to finance: **www.enterprisenation.com/marketplace**

Someone who has seen first-hand the benefits of outsourcing accounts – and other key functions – is Rob Welch of smallcarBIGCITY.

Name: **Rob Welch**

Business: **smallcarBIGCITY**

It was whilst attending an interview after leaving university that Rob Welch met a man who was soon to become his business partner.

"I got chatting with someone else who was attending the same interview and who shared my love of classic Minis. I told him about my idea for conducting tours of London for tourists in classic Minis. He loved it and happened to also know someone that might be interested in investing. Neither of us ended up getting the job for which we were being interviewed but three of us did end up putting money in a pot and getting to work on making the dream a reality."

smallcarBIGCITY was born and four years on what started as a partnership has become an amicable case of Rob running and growing the business on his own.

"My first business partner left after a year. He wanted a salary that was competitive for his age and job role but this couldn't meet the budget of the company at the time. An opportunity came up and we both decided it was the right thing for him to do, so I bought him out. My second business partner stayed with me until November 2012. We had worked side by side for over three years and I think we both just needed a change.

I am still good friends with both of them and could not have set the business up without them. It was a wonderful experience. As with any relationship, circumstances change and things have to evolve to progress. I learnt a great deal about partnerships. In the early days everything was settled with a gentleman's handshake, which is fine when you start with nothing but becomes trickier when you start making money. My advice would be to start on solid legal ground where everyone knows exactly where they stand, no matter how strong your friendship."

Rob and his co-founders received lots of press on launch as the product was unique and the founders were young so it made for a compelling story. Rob realised it was dangerous to sit back and rely on this initial exposure to carry the company, so to turn profile into profit, the company signed up to reseller websites and introduced an affiliate programme, approaching businesses that had access to the same demographic smallcarBIGCITY was after. The company did deals with boutique hotels, bars and restaurants and started targeting charities, offering tours as prizes for charity auctions.

"Marketing has moved so quickly over the last five years and I just don't think conventional advertising in newspapers, magazines and TV applies to small businesses with small budgets. What we do have on our side is a good story and renegade spirit! One of the most successful marketing campaigns we ran was targeting travel bloggers and journalists from all over the world and inviting them to sample the product for free. We took one Australian journalist round on a 1.5hr Italian Job tour and she wrote a lovely article in a major Sunday newspaper about us that resulted in approximately £40,000 worth of business in the space of three months."

In being the boss, Rob has come to appreciate the business benefits of focusing on what you do best and outsourcing the rest.

"When we first launched we had no money so tried to do everything possible in-house. We quickly found we were spending a huge amount of time teaching ourselves things that an expert would be able to do very quickly. I hate accounting and calculating tax liability, yet I would spend hours wading through information from HMRC, trying to work it out for myself. It took me about a year to realise that my time had a value and that it was far better spent sourcing new business and developing new corporate alliances.

Following this through, we now have 11 part-time drivers who are all self-employed. An administration assistant comes in once a week to keep the books in order and two interns focus on our social media campaigns and email shots. I subcontract the annual accounts and bookkeeping to a professional accountant. A marketing company takes on the ad-words campaign, email marketing and guerrilla impact campaigns.

My time initially was spent 60% admin, 30% tours, 10% growth. Subcontracting means that I now spend my time 20% admin and 80% growth. Since making this change our sales have increased by 30%."

The appetite for outsourcing also relates to advice from experts who Rob has met through four years of networking.

"I have built up a network of friends, everyone from lawyers to TV producers, who can pretty much answer any question I have. You do not need to be an expert in every industry; you just need to know someone who is."

These experts are having an input when it comes to advising Rob on how to grow the business. He's looking to scale up to a fleet of 100 cars, used for touring, film shoots, weddings and even treasure hunts. He sees potential in the self-drive hire business with new and old Minis and scope to expand into different cities across the UK. A new subsidiary company has been launched, Best London Tours, which resells the top 1% of attractions and experiences in London and the plan is to grow this venture by 40% over the next 12 months.

"With regards to global domination," says Rob, "the dream is to have VW Beetle tours in Berlin and Cadillac tours of

New York! The market has been proved, I just need to get London rocking and rolling so that I can free up the time to go and do it!"

You can bet this young entrepreneur will achieve his ambitions, with supporters closely in tow!

 www.smallcarbigcity.com

 @smallcarbigcity

Stay updated with your own accounts and alongside an accountant by using a software package. They are available in the cloud, meaning you can access accounts from any location and on any device. Here are the most popular options:

PRODUCT	COST/OFFER	LINKS
Intuit Quickbooks	*30-day free trial followed by three product offerings of £9/£19/£20 per month*	www.intuit.co.uk/quickbooks-accounting-software @QuickBooksUK
SageOne Accounts	*30-day free trial and £10 per month thereafter*	uk.sageone.com/accounts @sageuk
Sage One Payroll	*30-day free trial and £5 per month thereafter for up to five employees*	uk.sageone.com/payroll @SageUKHRPayroll

FreeAgent	*30-day free trial followed by £15 per month (sole trader), £20 per month (partnership) £25 per month (limited company)*	www.freeagent.com @freeagent
KashFlow	*14-day free trial followed by £18 per month*	www.kashflow.com @kashflow
Xero	*The company states a 'free trial and pay nothing until you're ready' – when you are, it's £19 per month*	www.xero.com @xero
Crunch	*Package of accountants and software for £59.50 per month*	www.crunch.co.uk @teamcrunch

The business may reach the point where you feel you need a part-time or outsourced Finance Director, in addition to the services of an accountant or software package.

There are companies that specialise in this, including the EFM Network (www.efm-network.com), The FD Centre (www.thefdcentre.co.uk) and FD Solutions (www.fdsolutions.uk.com).

"We have a group of highly professional associates across the UK (currently 25 and aiming to have 50 in the next two years) who can provide a Finance Director or Financial Controller service at a fraction of the normal cost. Essentially you buy in services as and when you need them versus paying top dollar for full-time FDs which you may not require."

JACKIE WADE, HEAD OF BUSINESS DEVELOPMENT, EFM NETWORK

Social media

Spend time managing your social media presence before handing it over to a specialist so you set the tone for the company and get an understanding of what works with customers and contacts.

Hootsuite (**www.hootsuite.com**) helps you manage your social media presence by scheduling tweets and posts and measuring their results. You are still carrying out the work in-house but making efficiencies with your time. Hootsuite is free to use for up to five social profiles, moving to $8.99 per month for five to 100 social profiles.

When it gets to the point that social media is taking up a little too much time, it's time to consider outsourcing these aspects:

- Creating profiles on the major social media platforms (Twitter, Facebook, LinkedIn, YouTube, Google+, Instagram, Pinterest)
- Managing profiles by publishing content and images, engaging in conversations and responding to customer enquiries

- Contributing posts to popular news sites and blogs in your sector
- Measuring what works

Carrying out this work reaps reward in the form of impressive search results when customers are searching for what you offer, i.e. an active social media presence improves your search engine optimisation or SEO. Find social media experts on talent marketplaces listed on page 168 onwards and check out these people I've met who have made social media their chosen specialist subject:

- Alicia Cowan – a certified social media and internet marketing specialist, Alicia delivers online training programmes and social media summer camps that help small business owners promote themselves online (www.aliciacowan.co.uk, @absolutealicia)
- Alison Battisby – a social media consultant, copywriter and blogger, Alison works with brands large and small through her own business, Avocado Social (www.avocadosocial.com, @alisonbattisby)
- Hallam Internet – founded and run by internet marketing expert Susan Hallam, the company offers services ranging from strategy to SEO, social media and paid search (www.hallaminternet.com, @hallaminternet)
- Luke Smith/Croud – Croud deploys a network of experts to take on the social media tasks you want to leave to the professionals (www.croud.co.uk, @croudmarketing)
- Mark Shaw – a Twitter expert and author, Mark can offer advice on how to tweet like a pro! (www.markshaw.biz, @markshaw)

- Michael Tinmouth – a pro when it comes to helping businesses, large and small, engage with customers via social media – and taking it offline too (**www.michaeltinmouth.com**, **@michaeltinmouth**)
- Warren Knight – a social media and digital commerce expert (**www.warrenknight.co.uk**, **@wvrknight**)

These experts can quickly pick up your tone of voice, engage an audience and, critically, manage and develop your social media presence.

Email marketing

Capture data from visitors to your website by asking people to sign up to a newsletter. This commits a contact to hearing from you and it commits you to sending a newsletter – or maybe more than one!

Outsource email marketing with software and to the companies that provide it such as Constant Contact (**www.constantcontact.com**), SignUp.To (**www.signup.to**) and iContact (**www.icontact.com**).

"It's rare for someone to become a customer as soon as they hear about you, so what you need to do is make it easy for someone to express interest in your business

> *and opt in to hear from you by email. It's then possible to create an automated sequence of messages – set at predetermined intervals – that lead someone through the process of learning about your business, realising the value and becoming a customer. This lets you put a key part of your sales process on autopilot!"*
>
> MATT MCNEILL, FOUNDER, SIGNUP.TO

Top tips on email marketing

John Hayes is a marketing strategist and author of two books including *A Crash Course in Email Marketing for Small and Medium-sized Businesses*. He says email marketing is still the most cost-effective marketing technique available to small businesses for driving repeat business. Here's how to go about it.

- **Build and send**
  - » Start building your email marketing list from day one. Acquire contact details in a number of ways including via a sale, a subscription to a list (newsletter) and face-to-face meetings (networking events, trade shows, etc.). The longer you leave an email address before contacting it, the more chance your message will be ignored or marked as spam. Bear in mind the average email address has a lifespan of approximately 18 months. Don't wait for your list to reach a critical mass before you start sending; lists with less than 100 names can still return significant results.

- **With permission**
  - Don't add names to your list who haven't given you permission to do so. This is spam and is highly likely to damage your reputation.
  - Buying lists is also not advised. No matter how the company has collected the data and secured the permission from its subscribers, there is no basis of permission between you and the email owner. Therefore a campaign sent to a purchased list will have all the hallmarks of spam.
- **In the right place and at the right time**
  - Email marketing works at its very best when it is targeted, timely and engaging. This means sending the right message to the right contact at the right time. As you build your list you will want to segment your contacts according to a number or criteria such as relationship (i.e. client or prospect), purchase type, gender, geography, etc. While the monthly newsletter still plays a significant role in small business marketing, email marketers will see more success if they send campaigns on a more regular basis to smaller groups of people.

> *"62% of companies now outsource their content marketing"*
>
> SOURCE: OUR SOCIAL TIMES (www.oursocialtimes.com/62-of-companies-now-outsource-their-content-marketing)

Sales

When you hear that on average it takes 80 calls to get an opportunity, you realise that's a lot of calls to make when you're also making product and keeping customers happy!

As with other tasks, take on sales yourself at first. Make the calls (and always do so whilst standing up and smiling as you will come across as confident and optimistic), attend shows, markets and sales events and meet clients to secure deals. Track this activity with a spreadsheet or tailored software such as Salesforce (www.salesforce.com).

When sufficient sales are coming in, dedicate budget to hire sales professionals, with you still having oversight and maintaining control. For sales and business development, the functions that can be outsourced include:

- **Data lists**
  - I'm a big fan of building your own database and business community but if you want to test a new product or market, data lists are available to buy from companies such as Experian (www.experian.co.uk/business-express/helping-grow-your-business/grow-overview.html) and the Royal Mail's Mailshots Online where you can build and send a direct marketing campaign to an acquired data

list, all managed from your own PC (www.royalmail.com/marketing-services-occasional/deliver-your-campaign/mailshots-online).

- **Telemarketing & lead generation**
  - Specialist companies such as Great Guns Marketing (www.greatgunsmarketing.co.uk) and PCM Telemarketing (www.pcmtelemarketing.co.uk) offer telemarketing services. These businesses can assist with making appointments, generating sales leads, follow-up calls from a marketing campaign and recruiting for events.
- **Sales teams for events**
  - This is usually outsourced to friends and family and friends of friends who can make the date! Or you can hire extra pairs of helping hands from event staffing agencies such as Hel's Angels (www.helsangels.net).
- **Agents and distributors**
  - When entering international markets, sales agents and distributors become your force on the ground and, in a similar way, consultants and franchisees act as sales representatives across the UK, with this being covered in detail in the Franchise section.

Online sales

Outsource online sales to third-party sites through a drop-shipping or affiliate relationship whereby the partner site promotes and sells the product and you ensure it's delivered to a happy customer. Affiliate sites include Affiliate Window (www.affiliatewindow.com), CJ (uk.cj.com) and Tradedoubler (www.tradedoubler.com).

Fashion brand Rapanui developed a drop-shipping system so they could effectively sell their desirable t-shirts via a selection of third-party sites.

Name: Rob Drake-Knight

Business: Rapanui

Started by two brothers with an interest in sustainability and a vision to eradicate youth unemployment on the Isle of Wight, Rapanui supplies t-shirts to young people across the globe. It started by combining a summer of savings.

Rob Drake-Knight says of himself and brother, Mart:

"We decided we wanted to 'do something' to make a contribution to sustainability so pooled our summer savings and bought a box of t-shirts which we sold to friends and family with the proceeds buying two more boxes. Our parents were supportive – allowing us the garden shed as our office! Other than that we didn't have a great deal of help with starting up the business."

Having started off buying blank garments, the brothers traced the supplier and then the factory so they could order direct and have more control over the production process. They also wanted to be in control of their sales channels so developed their own drop-shipping system.

"We started with a rudimentary system back in 2009 and have developed this to include stock feeds and product feeds – meaning we have very little administration. All orders from third-party sites get auto-filled into our orders database and management system. It works really well for us and the partner – they get to limit risk and we get to make sales. We work with some big name partners and some of the larger partners have moved onto wholesale from this system too."

The company is now selling overseas with 10% volume going to the EU, 5% to the United States and 5% to Australia with orders coming from Rapanui's own site after being found via search results and coverage in the media. The plan is to launch new products, increase marketing and expand at a faster pace overseas. It will test the online sales strategy to the max!

 **www.rapanuiclothing.com**

 **@rapanuiclothing**

PR

The question of whether to hire a PR agency or keep it in-house is one that many small business owners grapple with. Does a journalist prefer to hear from a known PR contact or get a story direct from the horse's mouth? When it comes to PR, as with sales, there are key components that make up a successful PR strategy. Here's the DIY approach:

- **Press release** – write your own release and upload to release distribution services such as SourceWire (www.sourcewire.com) which come with a template for you to complete and a cost of £50 to distribute the release to up to three categories of journalists or £75 for four to ten categories. Attaching images and video footage incurs further charges.

- **Imagery** – sort your own professional photography so that good-looking images can be attached with the release – and increase the chances it will be used.
- **Contacts** – knowing your customers means knowing the publications and blogs they read and online news sources they visit. Find media contacts at these publications and blogs through dedicated databases such as Gorkana (www.gorkana.com), which carries details of 165,000 journalists and bloggers.
- **Ongoing relations** – if a journalist carries your story, stay in touch and keep feeding your new contact with relevant comments, stories and stats.
- **Measurement** – evaluate the return on investment or ROI by signing up for a Google news alert (www.google.com/alerts) which will alert you each time you are mentioned online and measure the reach and significance of social media with Sprout Social (www.sproutsocial.com).

Your consideration is always a time and cost analysis. Ask yourself: should you be spending your time working on this activity, or outsource it to a professional who will take less time to write a release, has the contacts in his/her database to hand, and has the motivation to measure what's working as the results justify their work?

Pitching for PR

"PR is all about reputation. Having a good reputation opens doors, makes negotiations easier and quicker, and can increase the value of a company. In the early stages it can be helpful to get a summary from a seasoned PR person that describes your business. Getting an objective view from someone outside the company, who knows how to use language in a way that the media and the wider world understands, is vital.

To start with, commission a simple one-pager that will throw light on how the world sees what you do, how your business fits in the bigger picture and identify the things it needs to do to get noticed by the people who matter.

This basic information is invaluable. It can even influence the direction your business might take. The copy produced can also be used on your website and help form the basis of press releases and dialogue with journalists, helping you to identify points of difference and how to communicate them. Use it well and efficiently. This initial consultation should be inexpensive – and is worth every penny.

Once your business is at a stage where you need to start getting the message out with more force because you have more mouths to feed, find a PR company that will work on a project-by-project basis. They can devise the most effective campaign strategy that will work for you. Strategy could be as simple as targeting the consumer press, but it could work on many levels – B2B, consumer, financial and personal profile being raised all at the same time.

Outsourcing this element of strategy is an efficient way of working, especially for small businesses just taking flight."

Liz Slee, head of media, Enterprise Nation

Join Enterprise Nation and benefit from free consultation calls with sales, marketing and PR experts.

Outsourcing PR has worked for Victoria Cramsie as it has given her the time to focus on increasing the all-important turnover and profitability of her young business.

Name: Victoria Cramsie

Business: Paperboy Interiors

It was the personal experience of having two sons and not being able to find any 'nice' wallpaper that led Victoria Cramsie to believe there was a gap in the market for her product.

"I canvassed opinion from a number of interiors shops to check I was right that decent wallpaper specifically aimed at boys just didn't exist. I also have a group of eight people, from a variety of backgrounds and disciplines, who I use as a sounding board for ideas – they gave positive feedback too. Then I researched designs for boys on the internet and this confirmed there was an acceptance that good quality interior design for boys was lacking.

The recession and stagnation in the housing market has made a lot more families stay in the homes they are in, so they are focusing more on the details of the house. I also felt we had swung too far away from pattern – and wallpaper in particular – and that surely we must have got fed up with plain white walls! I had a feeling that wallpaper would be coming back into fashion pretty soon. It's too gorgeous to ignore for long."

The business was launched and Victoria started by keeping PR firmly in-house.

"In the beginning there wasn't the budget for PR so I managed it myself. I approached design blogs directly and had a good response at no cost. But after a while I couldn't deal with the number of image requests, and also felt I needed some guidance on photography and to have someone contact the magazines on my behalf to try and sell in stories. I found my PR company on Twitter – I felt this was an easy way to quickly get a feel for what agencies can do and you're able to see how they interact with clients. The company writes and distributes my releases but I oversee this as it's so important to me that all communications stay true to the 'tone of voice' of PaperBoy.

I now feel I need to spend more money on PR to sell not just the wallpapers and fabrics but the 'story' of the business. I also want to broaden PR to other countries as we sell worldwide."

The PR company applied their own expertise to get this start-up in the media, with a spotlight on the niche it served.

"Focusing on a niche and having a very clear and simple message has allowed us to get the message across of what we do easily and effectively. It's quite clear what we do from the name of the brand and also from the 'About' page on the website. There is no confusion as to who we are/what we do/what we make so I think this has made us quite a memorable brand for media and also to our customers. In terms of press coverage it helps too. A piece on decorating for boys ... who are you going to get in touch with ... PaperBoy (well, hopefully!)."

Victoria's job is to come up with the designs and initial drawings. She is now working with an illustrator who can quickly put on paper exactly what is in Victoria's head.

"I'm not a natural or trained artist so that has always been the stumbling block for me. To have access to a pair of quality drawing hands has made the process much simpler.

Having finalised the designs and colours, these are sent off to the wallpaper printer in Norfolk and the fabric printer in London. I think that to be a serious manufacturer one has to use the skills of professional (in this case) printers. There would be no point in me attempting to print wallpaper or fabric. They know what they are doing and it also means that the business is scaleable. They can print 100 rolls of wallpaper or 1,000. I can't imagine trying to do that in the studio here!

Someone gave me a great piece of advice at the outset: behave like the company you want to become, not the one you currently are. Invaluable advice when thinking of production."

Influenced by her sons at the start of this entrepreneurial journey, Victoria's boys continue to play a role.

"Unfortunately they haven't quite got to grips with issues of copyright and licensing and are dying for me to make a design based upon their favourite Xbox games. For colour they are very good; they are drawn to the more subtle, darker colours which is interesting to me. They also have a great sense of humour so if they don't think the 'joke' I am trying to convey in a design is a good one, I'm quite sure that they're right and I start to think again."

 **www.paperboywallpaper.co.uk**

 **@PaperBoyLondon**

Legal services

Who needs a whole department when you can outsource legal work to companies such as Rocket Lawyer, Off to See My Lawyer and legal experts such as Suzanne Dibble, who offers her views below on the legal arrangements to get in place when growing a business through outsourcing. Websites such as Clickdocs provide downloadable documents meaning you can be trading lawfully whilst still on a budget.

- Rocket Lawyer: www.rocketlawyer.co.uk, @rocketlawyeruk
- Off to See my Lawyer: www.offtoseemylawyer.com
- Clickdocs: www.clickdocs.co.uk
- Suzanne Dibble: www.suzannedibble.com, @law4onlinebiz

Admin

Outsource the jobs you don't want to do to the people who do! Save time by outsourcing diary management, travel bookings and the day-to-day operations of the business. Secure a Virtual PA on any of the talent marketplaces or via industry associations and dedicated websites including:

- UK Association of Virtual Assistants: www.ukava.co.uk
- Time etc: www.timeetc.com

- Worldwide101: www.worldwide101.com

Jane Field recognised she needed to outsource the detailed work. In fact, she's taking someone on so she can start working on the business, rather than in it.

Name: Jane Field

Business: Jonny's Sister

This is a global business run from an outbuilding in the grounds of Jane's house in scenic Somerset. I first met Jane when she was profiled in *Go Global*. Sending one of her highly sought-after love cushions to the Editor of *Country Living* was the break Jane needed. The cushion found its way into the Emporium pages of the magazine and the next thing Jane knew she was receiving orders from across the globe. Those orders still continue to this day.

"International sales are still growing. We get a fair amount (around 10% of overall orders) from our shop on **Notonthehighstreet.com** and the international sales we generate ourselves come either direct from the customer or a third-party retailer. If I had the time I would do more research on the European magazines with a view to getting featured as there is definitely a lot of potential. Germany, Spain, Denmark and Sweden work well for us, although it's interesting how each country favours different products. For example, Sweden just does not 'get' bunting at all!"

The business has grown to such a size that it is now employing five people full-time and four contractors. There's an ambitious plan to grow 40% over the next 12 months which Jane is looking to achieve through introducing new products.

"In coming up with new product concepts, we have to think like the customer. Everyone still has birthdays but maybe instead of spending £50 they can now only spend £30 but they do not want it to look like a £30 gift. We have made sure our offering suits this demand so you don't automatically know the product cost and as it's personalised the recipient thinks the person has spent time and effort on it. We are also responding to trends; our personalised enamel cake tins have done very well since the airing of *The Great British Bake Off*!"

Jane leverages technology to grow her business by having a presence on marketplaces such as **Notonthehighstreet.com** and making the most of virtual support to tap into the asset base of talented people who are at home with children, would love to work, yet can't necessarily leave the house for eight hours a day.

"I guess the secret to success comes down to being flexible and buying in expertise rather than employing it. Oh, and planning everything carefully which is why I'm looking for an office manager so I can stop working in the business and free me up to work on the strategy."

 **www.jonnyssister.co.uk**

 **@jonnyssister**

Talent scout

Online marketplaces play an increasingly important role when it comes to finding the talent you need to grow. In August 2013, oDesk reached a milestone of more than $1bn being spent by businesses and freelancers on the platform. The company has since merged with the next largest marketplace, Elance, to create the behemoth of the industry that analysts expect will rise to a market size of $5 billion by 2018.[2]

> *"With the Internet opening up access for businesses and professionals to work together, we're facing rapid change and a simple truth – work is no longer a place. As Facebook disrupted communications and eBay disrupted commerce, oDesk is disrupting the way we work. Online work removes friction by opening up a flexible, global talent pool – helping the best-matched businesses and workers find each other when demand exists."*
>
> Gary Swartz, CEO, oDesk

The most common talents and tasks UK businesses are looking for on these marketplaces include web programming and design, SEO (search engine optimisation), mobile apps, graphic design, web research and blog and article writing.

---

2 Staffing Industry Analysts via *The Economist*, 'The workforce in the cloud' www.economist.com/news/business/21578658-talent-exchanges-web-are-starting-transform-world-work-workforce

Top 10 sites on which to find the talent you're after

SITE	SIZE	SKILLS AVAILABLE
99 Designs www.99designs.co.uk	*242,273 creative designers*	*Designs for logos, web pages, business cards, mobile apps and just about anything else you want designing!*
Crowdspring www.crowdspring.com @crowdspring	*Referring to itself as 'The world's number one marketplace for logos, graphic design and naming', the site houses over 140,000 creatives*	*Logo and stationery design, web design and company names. 43 categories of skills in total*
Dribbble www.dribbble.com @dribbble	*Rather than a project marketplace as such, Dribbble is an online showcase for designers, showing small screenshots of what they're working on.*	*Web designers, graphic designers, illustrators, icon artists, typographers, logo designers.*

	SIGN-UP AND COST
	Complete an online design brief, pay for a design package starting at £199, increasing to gold package at £539. Each offer a set number of designs and 100% money back guarantee. Your brief is then posted in the marketplace and designers respond. In seven days, you pick the winner, the money is transferred to the designer, the copyright transferred to you and the completed design to download. Job done!
	You select the services you need from the categories, name your price and state the deadline. Freelancers then pitch to you. The average number of responses is 110 – once you've picked your favourite, you work with them on the design and pay when you're happy. The site offers a 100% money back guarantee.
	*There is a 'Find Designer' function on the site (*www.dribbble.com/designers*) and you have to sign up as a 'scout' to find and follow designers. You then contact designers direct from their profile.*

Elance www.elance.com @elance	Over 500,000 businesses and two million freelance professionals in more than 150 countries. The site claims one million freelance jobs are completed through Elance each year with $700 million earned since the site launched.	Writing, video editing, coding, photography, virtual admin, social media & customer service. In the first quarter of 2013, 40% of jobs posted were for creative skills, 39% for IT, 10% Marketing & 7% operations
Enterprise Nation	Almost 11,000 small business advisers have profiles on the Enterprise Nation marketplace and are awaiting your business	Advisers across five categories: Sales & Marketing, Access to Finance, Leadership & Management, IT and Web and taking on staff

	After registering for an account, it's free to post a job and you pay when the work has been approved. See interview below with UK country manager Hayley Conick for a detailed description of how the site works and payment processes.
	It's free for advisers to create a profile on the Enterprise Nation marketplace and small business members receive up to three free consultation calls as part of their membership. The marketplace has fast become the TripAdvisor for business support with advisers rated and reviewed.

Fiverr www.fiverr.com @fiverr	*Describing itself as 'the world's largest marketplace, for services starting at $5, Fiverr is a treasure trove of talent!*	*Graphic & design, musicians, video & animation, writing and translation, business planning and market research.*
Freelancer.com www.freelancer.com @freelancer	*With over 8 million users and over $1 billion worth of projects posted, Freelancer.com ranks alongside Elance and oDesk as one of the three largest marketplaces*	*Web design, copywriting, app development, coding, customer support, virtual admin*
Guru.com www.guru.com @guru_com	*Over 400,000 Gurus are displaying their skills for small businesses to access*	*Business consulting, graphic design, engineering, illustration & art*

	Fiverr has seen an increase in the number of companies coming onto the site to buy services as well as micro entrepreneurs being on the site to sell their services. You select the seller you want, based on reviews, ratings and portfolio and can communicate with the seller before you buy. Once you order, the money goes out of your PayPal account. Fiverr is known for being the marketplace where you'll find skills (and marketing ideas) that you might not find elsewhere, such as someone producing a company video with international locations as the backdrop or suggesting names for a new business.
	After signing up on the site, you post a project and only pay once satisfied with the work. It is free to post a project and liaise with freelancers but once a project is awarded, Freelancer.com takes a 3% fee on the value of the project awarded or you can sign up to a membership package and pay a range of fees depending on the package. Details of membership packages available at www.freelancer.com/feesandcharges/#projectupgrades
	As a company posting a project, you don't pay anything as Guru makes its money through charging freelancers a fee on the project. In using SafePay, the money does not get transferred to the contractor until you are happy with the work. The site directs users to Guru Answers – a community forum for questions on how the system works.

oDesk www.odesk.com @odesk	*With over three million registered freelancers, the site saw 1.5 million jobs posted in 2012. Since merging with Elance, the merged entity now represents the largest marketplace in the industry*	*Logo designers, WordPress experts, SEO specialists, translators, personal assistants*
Peopleperhour.com www.peopleperhour.com @peopleperhour		*Design, writing, web development, marketing & PR, social media*

	As the company clearly states: 'It is always free to sign up, post jobs, interview candidates and hire on oDesk. The freelancer rate you see already includes a 10% oDesk fee, so you pay nothing extra.'
	There are three ways of sourcing talent: Browse Hourlies, which are fixed-price offers from people ready to start immediately; you can post a job to which freelancers respond; or contact freelancers direct and request a proposal. You then review and accept proposals via a work system built into the site and only pay when you're happy with the work. As the one requesting the project, you don't pay a fee to Peopleperhour.com as this is built into the freelancer's fee.

ALL FIGURES CORRECT AT THE TIME OF WRITING

When it comes to the art of creating a concise and successful brief for your project, Hayley Conick, UK country manager for Elance, says:

> "Let freelancers know exactly what the project entails, what's expected, what skills you're looking for and any other details critical to the project. Be careful not to include confidential information that you wouldn't want shared publicly. Provide example files; this can be something you've worked on, or something on the web that's close to the job you have in mind. Look for a freelancer who has direct experience tackling projects closely related to your job and positive feedback and ratings from previous clients."

Tracey Corcoron of iPilates is a big champion for Elance having used the site since starting her business in 2009 with business partner, Julia Jackson.

> "We have outsourced most tasks that we can't do ourselves through Elance: web design, cart integration, PayPal integration, logo design, research and marketing. My tips for using Elance would be: spend time thinking about what you want and write a detailed brief, including how you will assess the success of the assignment. When sifting through the responses, discard those that have not taken time to read your requirements and then use the Elance tools to grade the responses, taking into account expertise levels, price quoted, customer satisfaction and location, if that is important."

If you'd prefer more of an in-person approach, follow the lead of Sharon Beck of Popcorn Box who, in response to a Tweet, told me: "I found my web and logo designer in the school playground!"

Hopefully now you have an understanding of all the tasks that can be outsourced, and to whom. Then it's simply a case of ensuring the arrangements and structure are all above board and the team operates in tandem.

Keeping it legal

When hiring freelancers, it's important to enter into a professionally-drafted agreement. Suzanne Dibble offers advice on what your agreement should contain:

1. An express assignment of intellectual property rights – many small business owners assume if they have paid for something (such as a logo or website content), they will own the intellectual property rights in what they have paid for. That isn't the case and unless there is an express assignment (using the right legal terminology), the freelancer retains ownership – leading to problems in using, trademarking, licensing and/or selling the relevant materials.

2. A non-solicitation of clients clause (especially where the freelancer performs the same services as you) so that your freelancer cannot go straight to your client and try to cut you out of the picture.

3. Confidentiality provisions and a non-compete clause to prevent your freelancer from taking your confidential information and know-how to set up a competing business.

4. Crystal clear payment terms including the amount to be paid, how the payment is to be calculated, when the payment is to be invoiced (ideally once you have received your payment from your end client), the period you have to pay the freelancer's invoice, whether VAT is payable on top of the stated amounts, whether expenses and materials are included in the fee, any payment milestones and exactly what triggers the next payment.

5. Where relevant, an obligation on the freelancer to take out and maintain insurance, such as professional indemnity insurance or public liability insurance.
6. An indemnity (a legal term for reimbursement) from the freelancer for anything that they do in performing (or failing to perform) the services that results in a liability for you.
7. An obligation on your freelancer to comply with all applicable laws, regulations and codes of conduct in performing the services.
8. A clause stating that the freelancer is a self-employed contractor and not an employee and an indemnity from the freelancer for any tax, fines and/or penalties in the event that it is decided by HMRC or the courts that the freelancer is in actual fact an employee and that you should have been paying employer's National Insurance contributions.
9. Termination provisions so you can terminate the agreement on a certain period of notice at any time and immediately if the freelancer breaches the terms of the agreement, fails to carry out the services to the required standard or in some way is likely to jeopardise your reputation.

 www.suzannedibble.com

 @law4onlinebiz

When is a freelancer not a freelancer?

From a tax and legal perspective, there are limits to how much work you can outsource to one person before HM Revenue & Customs (HMRC) considers the freelancer to be your employee and expects you to pay their tax and National Insurance. Emily

Coltman is chief accountant at FreeAgent. She outlines the difference between subcontractors and employees:

If you choose to outsource to a one-man or one-woman business, how do you know whether HMRC might consider that person is actually employed by you?

And, indeed, if you are providing services to clients, is there a risk that HMRC might think they're employing you?

What does it matter anyway?

HMRC get more money through the employer-employee relationship because there's no employer's National Insurance to pay on subcontractors' fees, unlike on employees' wages.

HMRC look through any contracts (a contract of service for an employee, a contract for services for a subcontractor) and examine the actual dynamic of the relationship between the two parties – and if they find it to be really an employer-employee relationship, they'll ask for more money.

If the quasi-employee is a sole trader, then it'll be the client who pays that extra. But if the quasi-employee trades through an intermediary (their own limited company, or partnership), it's that intermediary that's liable for the extra.

So it could be very important!

When might HMRC consider someone is really an employee?

They will look at the whole picture and consider the relationship between the parties.

In an employment situation, the relationship will be on a "master-servant" level, rather than a relationship of two equals.

What does a "master-servant" relationship actually mean?

There's no statutory definition of when someone will be an employee, but HMRC give a series of questions as a general guide to help establish the picture.

Here's a summary of what HMRC are looking for:

- Employees have to do the work themselves; subcontractors can hire someone else to do the work at their own expense.
- Employers tell their employees what to do, and where, when and how to do it, and move them from task to task. Subcontractors can decide this for themselves.
- Employees work a set number of hours; subcontractors only carry out work when they're needed.
- Employers are obliged to provide their employees with work, but there's no such obligation if the worker is a subcontractor.
- Employees are paid by the hour, week, month or year. Subcontractors are often paid a set fee for a job, regardless of how long it takes to do.
- Employees may receive overtime pay, bonus payments, holiday pay and sick pay. Subcontractors are very unlikely to be given any of these.
- Employees don't risk their own money in a business. Subcontractors do, but they can also derive a reward by making profit on a particular job. For example, a self-employed printer gets to keep more of his earnings if he can buy paper more cheaply.
- Employees don't have to correct any errors they make in their own time and at their own expense, but subcontractors would have to do this.

- Subcontractors often work regularly for a number of different people.
- Employers will provide equipment such as computers for their employees, but subcontractors will often provide their own equipment.

These are not hard and fast rules, though. For example, if an employee is hired because they are expert in their particular field, the employer may not exercise as much control as over a trainee employee.

HMRC will also look at whether a particular individual is "part and parcel" of the organisation. An email address at the organisation, business cards, and the individual describing themselves as part of the organisation, for example "I'm Emily Coltman from FreeAgent", is a pointer to employment.

HMRC do look at the whole picture rather than considering any of these factors in isolation – and having a contract for services in place rather than a contract of service is not enough on its own to point to self-employment. They look at the substance of the relationship.

These are points to bear in mind as you grow through 'recruiting' freelancers as opposed to full-time employees.

 www.freeagent.com

 @freeagent

Professional protection

When it comes to insurance and ensuring you and the company are protected if you are outsourcing work to freelance consultants and experts, both parties should have their own insurance. Take the example of a PR company outsourcing work for social media contracts to a freelance specialist. With regard to who has the responsibility to have professional indemnity insurance, James Gilmour, insurance relationship manager at Simply Business, says:

"Both groups of people need to be insured. If the consultant is a specialist in an area of PR that sits outside the business' usual practice, the company should ensure the consultant has their own coverage. In this instance it is worth making sure that the consultant has the same limit of coverage as the company."

 www.simplybusiness.com

 @simplybusiness

Talent manager

You are building a team of experts and specialists around you which comes with a requirement to manage the motivations of this talented and nimble workforce. What you're aiming for is a business that thrives on low overheads and flexibility, yet still carries a strong company feel so if anyone asked any of the team what the company stood for, they would each know and offer the same reply.

This can be achieved through effective communication and regular get-togethers.

- **Hook Up** – connect each day via email, phone, Skype and project management software so team members are aware of deadlines, daily activity and progress.
- **Meet Up** – get together, face-to-face as often as you need. In my business, we have a full team meet every month with weekly co-working and team members meeting more regularly

if particular projects demand it. The monthly team meet gives us the opportunity to catch up, plan, and come up with new ideas. They usually finish with a drink or two too!

> *"Ideas are bigger than offices – and the Enterprise Nation team has lots of them! Having a system that tracks progress on those ideas and being clear about goals and objectives helps everyone, wherever they work, feel part of the team."*
>
> San Sharma, Tech freelancer, Enterprise Nation

One company that has years of experience in cultivating a sense of unity amongst hundreds of self-employed individuals is Travel Counsellors. Founded by David Speakman, the company provides travel agency services across the globe. David outlines how the company creates shared values and a common purpose.

> "We have 1,209 Travel Counsellors (TCs) worldwide with 744 based in the UK and, amongst this community, strive to create a culture where everyone feels part of one business. This happens through TCTV (our own TV broadcast) with a daily TCTV show for company news such as offers, corporate travel deals, etc., weekly shows for each country and a monthly international show. TCs buddy up and get together on trips which we organise from HQ, such as a recent Family Day at Alton Towers for 400 people. Online message boards for TCs don't just cover travel advice – they cover general chat, charities they support, etc. Essentially, we create a community in which TCs protect each other and police the standards of the company and community. They feel a belonging and that they are part of something special."

Team spirit

When growing through outsourcing and subcontracting, you can mimic the actions of companies with full-time staff based in full-time premises, to generate that sense of one team and one spirit across the business. Here are some suggestions:

- Team page – profile your closest contractors on your website and highlight the contribution they make to the company
- Team input – use software such as Basecamp to source ideas and inspiration from a pool of talented people who offer the energy and expertise from delivering other contracts to suggest ideas to grow your business
- Team social – host meet-ups, away days and cultural get-togethers. Working with people with whom you enjoy social time is an added benefit and privilege.

If the business reaches a point where you have worked with another individual or company and feel there's a good fit, consider forming a partnership or joint venture to strengthen the ties, or employ them full-time!

Accelerate

Grow your small business by partnering with or selling to a big one! There's never been a better time to leverage the assets of large corporates to aid the growth of your venture. No need to employ space, people or systems when you can grow off the back of someone else's.

Big businesses in Britain have £388 billion sitting in their bank accounts and on balance sheets. With confidence returning to the economy, they are starting to spend and the good news for small business is they want to spend a chunk of it with you.

There are many reasons why corporates want to engage with companies like yours.

- **Access to talent** – large retailers, tech companies, service organisations, etc. want the fresh and modern products and services you offer – and they want your entrepreneurial energy to rub off on them too!
- **Associated goodwill** – as a small business you have provenance and a story that customers buy into. You are a brand and personality, shaking up markets with new products and approaches. By association, the big business benefits from the vibrancy and authenticity of your brand.
- **Safeguard the future** – one of the multinationals that has become a master at accelerating small ventures is Telefonica. Their UK CEO once told me the reason they invest in start-ups is because they'd rather have an interest in supporting their competitors of the future, as opposed to going up against them. Innovation and rapid prototyping comes from small business, and large ones are alert to the fact that any day now, you could be taking their customers. Better to have you in their team from the outset!

> *"Encouraging an entrepreneurial spirit among staff is vital to keeping companies forever youthful, according to experts in business psychology."*
>
> Kate Burgess, *Financial Times*, January 2014

Make the most of these motivations by making sales, entering competitions and seeking out opportunities to partner. The big businesses of Britain have plenty to offer in the form of space, people, finance and access to market.

PitchUp!

Big businesses increasingly want to buy from small. I have witnessed this first-hand with the PitchUp project we ran with Sainsbury's and John Lewis which saw shortlisted businesses present to buyers with a chance of securing life-changing contracts. A good number of them did!

In a May 2014 survey, we asked small businesses if they were selling – or wanted to sell – to big business. 55% of respondents said the intention was there but they weren't aware of the opportunities available or lacked contacts to approach.

Enterprise Nation has worked with the Department for Business, Innovation & Skills (BIS) to plug that gap and deliver a series of events – The Exchange – that match small businesses with buyers from big brands. So far we've covered the food, fashion and beauty sectors with participating brands including Tesco, Jaeger, House of Fraser, Topshop, Superdrug, Ocado, ASOS and Shop Direct.

Linda Anderson attended The Food Exchange to take her first steps to securing a contract with a national coffee chain.

Name: Linda Anderson

Business: Loafkins

It was on returning home after a delivery of cupcakes and loaf cakes to the local deli that Linda Anderson came up with her eureka idea.

"I was questioning if the popularity of the cupcake may have peaked, and at the same time thrilled with sales of my lemon drizzle and hummingbird loaf cakes. As I wondered what the Next Big Thing in cake might be I was inspired to fuse the two into something individual and unique. The name Loafkins popped into my mind and a thorough online search later I was delighted – if surprised – to see that no one else was doing this."

Loafkins are bigger than cupcakes, ideal for slicing and sharing and available in individual pods making them the perfect convenience cake.

For Loafkins to be successful there was a good deal of product development to be done, followed by market research, sampling and building sales and orders.

"Existing customers received discounted prices as they tested the cakes and also their postability. Cafés were offered samples and generous wholesale discounts to get Loafkins onto the counter for their own customers to taste. Boxes were sent to offices, companies and retail stores, with requests for feedback. Many tweeted their support and delight in the deliciousness of the cakes and the novelty value. Without exception the response was favourable.

A simple website was set up (**www.loafkins.com**) and linked to the parent company (**www.filledwithlovecupcakes.org**). The Filled With Love newsletter began to mention Loafkins and curiosity was roused as people clicked the links to the website and discovered more. Orders started to come in."

At this point Linda submitted a trademark application to protect the brand and prevent others selling similar products using the unique Loafkin name or logo.

"The big breakthrough was without a doubt my attendance at an Enterprise Nation day for food entrepreneurs. At just £40 for a day with buyers from Waitrose, Sainsbury's and Ocado, success stories from the likes of Jimmy's Iced Coffee, and media advice from my favourite magazine *Woman and Home*, it had to be money well spent!

It was indeed. I arrived, nervously, with my sample box of Loafkins. The tasting table was bedecked with amazing-looking products clearly further down the production and packaging line than my little cakes! I popped them on the table but they struggled to hold their own amidst so many glossy boxes!"

Impressed by the company's commitment to the local community and use of local suppliers, Nick Tolley, founder of Harris + Hoole, was one of the speakers Linda particularly wanted to hear.

"He impressed me greatly and I was keen to speak to them. Several people were waiting in a line for the company's buyer. I boldly asked if I might email her and grabbed a sticky toffee and salted caramel Loafkin and asked her to try it. She promised to do so and told me to speak to the manager of my local Harris + Hoole.

At 8am the following morning I did just that. I called the store only for the manager to answer the phone. I introduced myself but she had already heard of me and Loafkins and a meeting was arranged.

Samples baked and delivered, tasting and a few spreadsheets later we had a deal. Paperwork and policies were necessary and head office approval took a little while to come through but the official launch is now imminent with an in-store launch in the Rickmansworth branch of Harris + Hoole on May 31st."

This is one happy lady who is about to get her product in a good number of new hands.

 **www.loafkins.com**

 **@lindaaanderson**

You've got to be in it to win it

In January 2014, Ocado launched 'Britain's Next Top Supplier', a competition backed by top retailer Sir Stuart Rose and celebrity chef Tom Kerridge, to find a new supplier who would win a six-month listing and support through Ocado's marketing, social media and PR channels to the value of £10,000.

"At Ocado we believe in nurturing British suppliers, so we've made it our mission to source the UK's very best small producers. We love discovering exciting new products for our customers to enjoy."

The competition lasted three months and attracted over 400 entries. Winner, Hiver Beers, was announced in March 2014.

Expect to see many more competitions of this nature as big companies seek out your talent and innovations. Be on the lookout!

Make your pitch

Respond to opportunities with a professional pitch that shows comprehensive knowledge of your product and customers – and how you will help the large company reach and sell to more of them. Know your figures and at what price you can offer different volumes, as well as timescales for delivery.

Rekha Mehr (**@pistachio_rose**) is a former commercial buying manager for Amazon and Waitrose and has secured listings in Fortnum and Mason for her own business, Pistachio Rose. Rekha advises small businesses on how to pitch to big retailers and offers her top five points of preparation.

1. Approach

Find names of buyers through the trade press as they are often asked to write about or comment on category trends.

Avoid making contact on Mondays (certainly the mornings) which are typically spent preparing for internal meetings.

Not getting a response from the buyer you've approached? Try other members of the team like the assistant buyer or buyer's admin assistant who can advise you on a better time or way to get in touch, or move things forward themselves.

2. Presentation

Send a brief email which takes no longer than 60 seconds to read and communicates what problem your product is solving and why it's right for their customers.

Include any awards, high-profile endorsements or press coverage that you have received as testimonials speak volumes.

Follow up with a phone call 2–3 days later to ask how the buyer would like to take things forward; would they like you to email over more information, schedule a call, or book in a meeting?

3. Competitors

Understanding your market place, acknowledging your competitors and highlighting your unique position against them is imperative to success.

A unique selling point (USP) is the key reason that customers purchase so be sure to highlight it to your buyer whether it's cheaper, better value or the first of its kind. Don't be tempted to bad-mouth competitors as it will weaken your argument. Instead focus on the things that your product does best and let the facts speak for themselves.

4. Pricing

It's not essential to mention cost price in the first communication but you could mention the suggested selling price to help set the scene.

Negotiation must be a win-win for both yourself and the buyer, so ensure you know how low you're prepared to go.

Ensure you factor all costs in to your margin like delivery (buyers will not like to see this as an additional charge), a marketing allowance (to partake in their activities) and payment terms (often an extra discount is offered for prompter payment so factor this in upfront).

5. Add-ons

Buyers will expect you to be conducting your own marketing activity to promote the brand once it's on the shelves so be prepared to share your plans around that.

It's important to build a marketing budget into your own margin to cover additional activity like sampling/demonstrations or features in their publications.

Exclusivity isn't always a bad thing! Choose your first customer wisely and perhaps agree to a time limit which gives you some breathing space to focus on your next customer.

"I see all new suppliers as potential partners so a perfect pitch to me is one that convinces me there is a trusted relationship in the offing. The pitch needs to be perfectly timed, confident and engaging, well-prepared with samples, financial detail, provenance and production capability all worked into a compelling but honest pitch, which leaves me excited and assured about the reasons to buy and convinced by the potential partnership that lies ahead."

Anna Rigby, Head of Buying, Home Accessories, Gifts and Seasonal, John Lewis

Sell to government

Government spends £230bn every year on products and services across all layers: central government, local government, the police, NHS, emergency services, etc. Did you know there is a target that 25% of this should be spent with small businesses by May 2015? That's equal to an extra £75bn of contracts up for grabs for small business.

If you thought that spend only goes on big-ticket items like roads and rail, think again. Across the annual spend, the government buys:

- IT services
- facilities management like plumbing, cleaning, landscape gardening
- catering
- uniforms
- stationery
- taxi services.

You name it – the government is buying it!

To make it easier for small businesses to identify and apply for contracts, there's an online portal Contracts Finder (**www.contractsfinder.businesslink.gov.uk**) which has links with LinkedIn so you can form groups to bid and you will also be able to see how previous contracts were awarded, and at what price. You can search by postcode to view opportunities in your area and, on securing a contract, government commits to paying within 30 days – and will do its best to ensure large suppliers do too if that's the way you've chosen to secure a contract.

Here's advice from Sally Collier, head of Crown Commercial Services, on how to make the most of this significant opportunity:

- Determine your strategy, i.e. do you want to sell to central or local government and do you want to sell direct or via a large supplier?
- Based on this, decide on the top six relationships you need to cultivate, i.e. with large suppliers or direct with the buyers listed on Contracts Finder.
- Talk to the buyers! They want to talk to you to explain what they're after with the contract to ensure everyone gets the best result.

We are calling the opportunity to sell to government 'the biggest sales opportunity of the year for small business' – make moves now to make the most of it!

Partner up

On awarding you a contract, the big company wants to help you deliver and succeed. Mentoring from their employees on everything from production to packaging and pricing is likely to be on offer. Accept all the support you can!

Chilli sauce maker, Mr Singh's, went through the pitch process live on national TV before accepting the company wasn't in a position to deliver. Learning from the experience, they are now selling with confidence in major supermarkets, independent retailers, and across the globe.

Name: Kuldip Sahota

Business: Mr Singh's Sauce

The story of Mr Singh's Sauce began in 1985.

"My Dad started making the sauce for family and friends. He continued doing this at home and in the early nineties began to bottle a few jars, getting some labels made, and trying to sell to local shops. It was November 2008 when I spotted what he was trying to do and booked a £1000 stand at the BBC Good Food Show in Kensington on my credit card. We then had a frenetic nine days during which the sauce recipe was actually written down, scaled to 1000 units, bottled and sold boiling hot in the jars!"

Kuldip was able to pay back the money borrowed on his card and the family went on to do five more shows.

"We quickly started to gain a following (probably because we were this loud family selling chilli sauce!). We were invited to apply for the TV show *High Street Dreams*, and then selected. They filmed from January to March 2010 with the show airing on May 11th 2010 (we probably had a total of 4–6 months business experience by this time). Live on the show, we secured a contract with Asda and hit the shelves in November 2010.

After six to eight months we realised the relationship was not right. We were struggling to make the product on a larger scale (even going from 1000 to 4000 jars took weeks of planning), we were all working in full-time jobs and had no idea what it took to make the relationship work with one of the 'Big 5'. From this, we decided to halt the listing and concentrate on getting our packaging and production organised. Bearing in mind we had gone from a home-based business to Asda overnight, there was a lot of learning to do.

A lot of the research we did during the TV show turned out to be faulty because it was so rushed. By taking a step back, we secured Harvey Nichols and Selfridges, built a loyal retail following, and focused on the brand."

The company is now selling to supermarkets across the globe, with the founding team having been influenced by investors and giving thought to what they wanted the business to be.

"During this whole experience I was earning a lot and when I decided to give up my job, my savings dried up as I had to live on them and fund the business. This forced me to look at the business in a different way as I learned if this was to work it would need my full-time effort and far more liquidity than I had, as well as a business partner or mentor who actually understood business rather than my 'learn-as-you-go' method.

Once an investor and mentor had been found, I had to elevate the way I ran and understood the business because this was what was expected as standard by my investors.

Secondly, we made the decision to be owners of a brand, not a manufacturing business. It was critical for us to find a production partner who wanted to make our products THE EXACT same way as we made it at home. Finding this partner was a trial and error process. Think of it this way, how often will you marry the first person you meet? Almost every manufacturer you speak with will say yes, be your best friend, brew you a cracking cup of tea and be eager to do the job for you – only one will deliver! In our experience, it pays to spend time shopping around and drinking many cups of tea.

By outsourcing production, it allowed us the freedom to sell and market our business, brand and story. This, in turn, gave us liberty to approach bigger customers, armed with (self-gained) knowledge of what our own capabilities were and why working together would be beneficial for them. We outsource to a co-packing partner we know and trust. They understand our ambitions and want to grow with us; in fact, we told them at the beginning we would be their biggest customer soon and I believe we are getting close!"

In outsourcing production, Kuldip has freed up his time to focus on building the brand and the business. For this, he has ambitious plans for the next 12 months.

"My goals are to launch three new products, increase the number of independent retailers we have from 300+ stores (gained in 17 weeks) to 1000 stores, increase the number of Tesco stores selling to over 100 (we recently sold out with them), secure a second round of funding for future growth, attract more national media exposure and open the first Mr Singh's Chilli Shop and Delicatessen."

This business has learnt fast that the way to grow is through outsourcing to trusted experts and partners. It will continue to grow, selling sauce across Britain and beyond, by recruiting selectively yet still creating wealth for partners. Go, Mr Singh's!

 **www.mrsinghssauce.co.uk**

 **@mrsinghssauce**

Move In

Apply to a corporate-backed accelerator and benefit from space, funds, access to market and intensive mentoring. Here are seven London-based accelerators that appeal to sectors ranging from digital to retail and fast-moving consumer goods.

ACCELERATOR	BACKED BY
IDEALondon	*Cisco and DC Thompson are supporting digital and new media companies in this space in Shoreditch. Tenant Jenny Griffiths, founder of SnapFashion, says her route to market is being significantly accelerated via connections of the corporate backers – and peer support from fellow tenants is vital too.*
Collider	*'An accelerator dedicated to startups which help brands understand, engage with and sell to customers' – start-ups spend 12 months in this programme and benefit from links with supporting brands including Unilever and Haymarket.*
Iris Ventures	*Creative agency Iris is backing employees with bright ideas, as well as accepting entrepreneurs from outside the business. Benefit from creative mentoring – and access to the Iris client base which includes Samsung, Mini, Adidas and Domino's.*
Level39	*An accelerator with fine views, located on the 39th floor of Canada Square in Canary Wharf. Focused on start-ups with financial or retail technology products, you apply for membership and benefit from co-working with large IT companies and potential investors.*

	LINKS
	www.idea-london.co.uk @idealondon
	www.collider.io @collidergb
	www.irisnation.com @irisworldwide
	www.level39.co @level39cw

The Bakery	*With support from BMW, Heinz, Unilever, Stella Artois and more, The Bakery offers access to customers. You should have an idea for a marketing or communications technology. If chosen, you receive a budget of £50,000 and 8 weeks in The Bakery space to develop the product. If successful, access to market is through access to the big brands.*
TrueStart	*An accelerator focused on retail and consumer technologies, backed by Land Securities and Accenture. It provides space, capital and mentors with deep know-how and contacts.*
Wayra	*Telefonica has some serious global firepower and their accelerator offers funds, space, access to support and mentors as well as more than 300 million Telefonica customers in exchange for 10% equity.*

Matt Truman's accelerator is focused on the retail sector and backed by big brands including Land Securities and Accenture. Matt outlines the benefits to the big business backer – and the accelerated small business owner.

What gave you the idea for TrueStart?

I wanted to see the leaders and businesses of tomorrow before my competition and wanted to create a culture of entrepreneurialism within the True Capital Group.

When we examined the other incubator/accelerator offerings, we concluded there wasn't a sufficient option for retail start-ups and there were few who genuinely connected large with small. With our years in the retail sector, we felt we could bring this experience to bear so built our own hub.

	www.thebakerylondon.com @TheBakeryLDN
	www.truestart.co.uk @truestartuk
	uk.wayra.org @wayrauk

How many businesses can you accommodate and accelerate at any one time?

We accommodate 20 start-ups per year in our 5,000 sq. ft office in London's Victoria district, the heart of retail's west end, a place in itself that is embarking on huge innovation and regeneration via Land Securities' £2bn infrastructure investment. In flow terms, we currently receive 20–30 applications a week.

What kind of support do small businesses receive?

Businesses receive six months in our world-class space (I can't understand how anyone can launch and begin to build a business properly in 2–3 months), free legal, accounting and recruitment advice from our partners, dedicated day-to-day mentorship from our internal team and external sector specialist mentors plus access to our networks which have been built from 15 years building businesses in the retail and consumer industry.

Our finance package is flexible. To date we have written cheques between £25k and £50k but we also accept warrants for later stage companies who are well-financed but really need our network access to accelerate.

Big companies such as Land Securities and Accenture are backing TrueStart. What return do they get from their involvement?

Large companies need structured access to innovation to help retain or enhance their competitive advantage, and smaller companies need the acceleration large industry stakeholders can provide.

From the very beginning I wanted more than just a list of sponsors on a web page – I wanted integrated partners. In terms of return, our partners receive access to innovation ahead of its competition. Even if not acquiring or implementing the start-ups into their business, seeing the ever-faster changes ahead of their peers has, in our eyes, significant value to the head of strategy, head of retail or indeed the CEO.

During the set-up discussions of TrueStart, what also became clear was the cultural benefit we would bring. Executives from the partner companies are also mentors in the hub which brings cultural benefits back into their organisation. The side benefits of being associated with young, thriving businesses alongside investing in the future of the UK economy clearly generates positive messages but fundamentally it is about creating competitive advantage for the big business.

"The launch of JLAB represents something unique in the UK retail sector, giving businesses access to mentors and an environment where they can develop their ideas."

STUART MARKS, ENTREPRENEUR AND PARTNERING WITH JOHN LEWIS ON JLAB

Whether selling to, partnering with, or being accelerated by a large company, consider this a viable option as a route to growth.

In support of Growth

Growth Vouchers were launched by the government in January 2014 as a £30 million project offering access to strategic advice for growing businesses. A business owner receives up to £2,000 from the government, to match with their own money and be spent on an accredited adviser in areas from raising finance to making the most of digital technologies.

Enterprise Nation has developed the marketplace to which businesses are directed to find an adviser. Its build and development would not have been possible without the support of eight global brands (Citrix, Constant Contact, EDF Energy, Regus, Sage, Simply Business, Toshiba and Vodafone) who not only funded development but also promote the marketplace to their collective network of over one million small business customers.

These brands are playing a key role in helping growing businesses access the advice they need, in a way that saves the business owner both time and money.

 **www.enterprisenation.com/marketplace**

Part III: Support

As the business grows, surround yourself with the support required to ensure success. This involves connecting with mentors, embracing technology, finding the space to grow, and securing any finance required.

People

Mentors

An asset that will stand you and the business in good stead as it goes through growth is quality people. As expressed in many of the earlier pages of this book, this doesn't necessarily mean people you hire full-time.

Mentors can play an invaluable role and there are two types you're after:

1. **The sounding board** – this is the trusted contact who listens as you talk, enabling you to come to your own conclusion and decisions.
2. **The active adviser** – this is the entrepreneur who has been there and done it and wants to help and advise based on their own experience.

Find your ideal mentor(s) through active networking. Andy Law is a proven entrepreneur and mentor and has advice for business owners looking for their perfect match.

> "One of the most important things an entrepreneur can do is network. Keep meeting people all the time, and not just people in your business category. Networking gets you thinking, it contextualises what you are doing and you meet interesting people.
>
> It's the best way to find a mentor – particularly if you are networking through formal business associations. If you are looking for a mentor, consider the following:
>
> 1. What skills do you personally lack?
>
> 2. What expertise does your business lack?
>
> 3. What help do you need in your marketplace?
>
> The best mentors add specific help to do just one of these three.
>
> Look for someone with proven success and someone you feel comfortable being with.
>
> How you interact is important too. I find it best when it's structured."

Strategic advisers

Find strategic help on the Enterprise Nation marketplace, which is home to over 10,000 advisers from across the UK. Search by location or the kind of advice you're after with a range of expertise covered from sales and marketing, to accessing finance, and making the most of digital technologies.

Advisers are rated and reviewed, with the most reviewed appearing higher up in the search results. Join Enterprise Nation and benefit from three consultation calls with selected advisers.

 **www.enterprisenation.com/marketplace**

Investors

Investors can also be a source of advice – and contacts – to build business growth. See page 229 for details on where to find them.

Growth Accelerator

With its claim to be 'where ambitious businesses go to grow', the Growth Accelerator is a £190 million government-backed programme to offer growing businesses advice, mentoring and coaching. Businesses with up to four employees pay £600 to enrol on the programme and are matched with an adviser and support. One of the programme's beneficiaries is Clippy McKenna, founder of conserve and chutney maker, Clippys.

"Our coach on the programme was amazing – and a task master. He helped us think about how we could grow our business to supply the supermarkets. This had a profound effect on our business. Without the help of the programme, we wouldn't be where we are today."

 **www.growthaccelerator.com**

 **@growthaccel**

Technology

The technology is in place to make it perfectly possible to run your global and growing business from the spare room – soutsourcing work to fellow professionals and maintaining a professional image for clients. You have built your virtual team and everyone is working from home offices/coffee shops/on the move – with documents and operations hosted in the cloud. Here are ten apps you can use to manage this entrepreneurial workforce.

1. Email

Top of our list, but with a word of warning: email can be a virtual workforce's best friend or its worst enemy, depending on how it's used. If overused, it loses its effectiveness almost completely – messages get lost in a deluge and team members can get overwhelmed and then demotivated. Think carefully about copying people into messages – do they really need to take part in the discussion? Pick your subject lines wisely too. It will help you refer back to messages in the future. If the topic of a conversation has changed, change the subject line or start a new thread.

2. Basecamp

Email's great for some conversations, but for managing a project with a virtual team, it's hard to beat a dedicated project management app, like Basecamp. For one, it keeps your inbox free of clutter, hosting focused discussions on a dedicated project web page that your whole team can see. You can track progress towards a goal and manage to-do lists to help your team get there on time. You can share calendars, files and collaborate on documents too.

As with any software, the old adage applies: garbage in, garbage out. As long as you use sensible naming conventions for discussions and files, contribute to the right discussion threads rather than starting new ones, and know when to use email instead of project management software, Basecamp is a winner. Think of it as a living document of your teamwork.

 www.basecamp.com

3. Highrise

Made by the same people who make Basecamp, Highrise is a web-based contact manager to help you keep tabs on all your customers and suppliers. Why is it on this list? For virtual workers who spend time talking outside of their own team, it's essential. It helps everyone understand what was discussed, what the progress of proposals and deals are, and when they should next get in touch.

Let's say a member of your team can't make an important call with a potential client. As long as their Highrise notes are up-to-date, you can pick up that conversation with ease. In any case, it's useful to have your contacts hosted in the cloud and accessible from anywhere.

 www.highrisehq.com

4. Google Drive

Google Drive is the new home of Google Docs, which is Google's answer to Microsoft Office: word processing, spreadsheet and presentation software, free and available for all, in the browser.

The real benefit for virtual teams is the ability to collaborate on documents in real time. You can actually see the flashing cursors of your team members as you work together on a written document, a spreadsheet or presentation. You can leave comments on your team's work or chat, in real time, while you work together. And because it's all hosted in the cloud, it's available from anywhere, and constantly backed up.

 drive.google.com

5. Skitch

When you collaborate in a virtual team, it's sometimes easier to show rather than tell. Skitch is the solution in this scenario. It lets you quickly take a screen grab and annotate it with shapes, arrows, quick sketches and text. It's great when working on visual projects, like building a website, and it really helps you get your point across in fewer words, saving time and frustration.

 www.evernote.com/skitch

6. Join.me

Another app for show-don't-tell scenarios, join.me lets you share your screen with up to 10 other users, lets them control your computer, chat and swap files. It's sort of magical how quick and easy it is to do this – and it's great for showing work in progress or for helping out team members with technical difficulties that are hard to explain over the phone or by email.

 www.join.me

7. Skype

For day-to-day communication with your team, Skype is an essential app to have. Not only does it allow you to call and video call your team members for free, it's a really easy way to instant message one another and swap files directly. We use it in our team for quick conversations and to let each other know when we're working and where we're working, which just helps us feel like we're together, even if we're miles apart!

 www.skype.com

8. Evernote Business

In a virtual team, when you can't share an actual filing cabinet, Evernote is the next best thing – in fact, it's even better. You can capture, browse, search and share anything important to your business. You could use your Evernote account as a sort of company-wide 'wiki', so team members can document their work and update that documentation for others, now or in the future.

 www.evernote.com/business

9. Dropbox

For your business's output – its documents, photos and other files – store them safe and secure in the cloud with Dropbox. With Dropbox software installed on your team's computers, files are automatically updated, so everyone has the latest version, and they're backed up too, so you won't have to worry about losing your stuff.

 www.dropbox.com

10. iDoneThis

In between contact from team members, it can be easy to feel that no work is being done. This is a crisis of faith that needs to be overcome, but it does take some time – and, crucially, trust.

In the meantime there's iDoneThis, a simple web app that's more about celebrating your team's achievements than it is about spying: it sends an evening email reminder that everyone on your team writes a quick reply to saying what they did that day – just one line per task. The next day, everyone gets a digest with what everyone else has been working on.

It's really simple to use and gives you a nice overview on what's happening in your growing virtual team, and your growing business.

 www.idonethis.com

Here's a summary of the tech tools we use at Enterprise Nation and the role they play in helping us grow the business.

PRODUCT	**PURPOSE**
Basecamp	*Project management software that keeps the team in touch and deadlines met*
GoToWebinar	*Live webinars that attract new and existing visitors to the site*
Dropbox	*Moving and storing files is stress-free with this service in the cloud*
Eventbrite	*Manages event bookings and sales receipts*
Hootsuite	*Scheduling social media so we can encourage the community to engage when team members are otherwise engaged!*
Mailchimp	*Email system that powers the weekly e-newsletter as well as the StartUp email course (and hopefully a growth one to follow!)*

Stripe	*With small businesses joining Enterprise Nation and paying by Stripe, this forms part of our accounting and financial checks*
Ruby on Rails	*The platform that powers Enterprise Nation! And our content management system too*
Skype	*Instant messaging with the team and video calls when we're home-based and wanting a shared office feel (but can turn it off when we like!)*
Zendesk	*Manages customer and support queries*

Matthew Stibbe's business enables companies to carry out routine admin online, so you would expect this business owner to embrace technology to help him grow what he refers to as a 'little big business'.

Name: Matthew Stibbe

Business: Turbine HQ

"I originally had the idea for Turbine HQ when I was CEO of a software company in the late 90s. As the company grew the amount of paperwork grew as well. It felt like we were reinventing the wheel and wasting more and more time on bureaucracy."

Turbine was built as a platform to help businesses manage this bureaucracy and work more effectively.

"I have an office at home and I run TurbineHQ.com from there. Other staff work from home and our developers work from an office in Ukraine. I used to feel a bit awkward about it – you know 'running a business from home' sounds a bit lightweight – but then I remembered that the US president and our prime minister also work from home. Also, my morning commute takes me a minute or so!

We have customers in the US, Canada, Australia, New Zealand and, nearer home, in the UK (of course) and Ireland. We also have one in Thailand and Switzerland! We can support them all from the UK and as Turbine is an online application, they can access it anywhere. We offer online chat, phone and email support so there can be a bit of time zone juggling but it seems to work out okay.

The company is equivalent to five to ten full-time employees, depending on how much testing and graphic design is going on, but I run it like a one-man multinational."

When asked what his single favourite tech tool is, Matthew replies:

"Turbine is built on a whole raft of cool stuff and it's hard to pick just one. I don't want to get too abstract here but I think the most important thing is what you might call 'social technology' – the ability to work virtually and remotely with colleagues in different parts of the country and around the world is essential to Turbine. It would have been very, very difficult 20 years ago but now we can do it thanks to the internet."

www.turbinehq.com

@turbinehq

"Working remotely gives you that one big thing you need more than anything – time to get stuff done. Open lines of communication, a clear picture of where you're heading, a stream of consciousness on Basecamp combined with the occasional super-charged ideas splurge means we all know where we're going and how we're going to get there."

Liz Slee, head of media, Enterprise Nation

Space

You are looking for space in which to host team meet-ups, meet clients or hold events. Good news: a multitude of co-working spaces have opened to service the home business owner looking for out-of-home office space or grow-on space. Locate spaces on directory sites such as NearDesk, Desk Union, and Hubble HQ or consider a membership which gives you access on a regular basis.

The Third Space

"As a third space, between traditional and home offices, co-working spots are great. They attract communities of like-minded people with enough professional variety to make sparks and opportunities fly; organisers usually put on events for networking, training and exhibition, and you don't have to worry about your laptop when you use the bathroom or step outside."

WORKSHIFTING www.workshifting.com/2012/06/how-to-set-up-your-own-pop-up-co-working-space.html

Space directory websites

- NearDesk – purchase a card for £20 a year (per person) and have access to the spaces on the NearDesk platform (www.neardesk.com)
- Deskcamping – find a desk near you ... or maybe a few. There's also a section for work cafes (www.deskcamping.com)
- Desks Near Me – work and desk space available around the world, at the click of a mouse (www.desksnear.me)
- Desk Union – co-working space in the heart of Edinburgh
- Hubble HQ – connecting start-ups in London to available space (www.hubblehq.com)
- Workhubs – no longer being updated (as the founder went on to open a workspace!) but still has a live search function (www.workhubs.com)
- WorkSnug – an app that reviews workspaces so you don't have to – pointing out places with work environments, good wireless and tasty coffee (www.worksnug.com)

Here are 15 co-working spaces that show what's on offer.

COMPANY	LOCATIONS
3Space	*Nationwide*
Bizspace	*110 locations in England and Scotland*
Central Working	*London (various locations)*
Club Workspace	*London*
Electric Works	*Sheffield*

	WHAT'S THE DEAL	LINKS
	A charity that takes on empty space from large corporates and government and opens it to small social enterprises and charities on a temporary basis, and at no cost, i.e. if your business has a social purpose, you could secure workspace for free but may be given seven days notice to leave!	www.3space.org @3spaceorg
	Space on offer includes offices, creative studios and workshops.	www.bizspace.co.uk @bizspaceuk
	Memberships range from £99 to £449 per month depending on the number of times you'll visit and length of stay.	www.centralworking.com @centralworking
	Part of the publicly-quoted Workspace Group, one of the benefits of becoming a Club Workspace member is having access to a network of spaces in which to touchdown and work across London. Three types of membership package at £200/300/400 per month.	club.workspacegroup.co.uk @clubworkspace
	Focused on creative, digital and media businesses, membership is £50 per month which offers 24/7 access to communal areas of the space.	www.electric-works.net @electricworks

eOffice	*London*
Indycube	*South Wales (5 locations across Cardiff, Newport, Swansea)*
One Alfred Place	*London*
Regus	*Worldwide*

	With one office in London, annual membership is £99.99, giving access to over 140 centres worldwide and discounts to over 600 airport lounges.	www.eoffice.net @eOffice
	Become an associate member (£150 per month for full-time and £50 per month part-time) for access to all venues or pay as you go for £10 per day.	www.indycube.com @indycube
	One of the first of its kind in offering a stylish space for home business owners wanting to convey a professional impression to clients. New members have to be proposed by an existing member. Fees are circa £1,500 for annual membership.	www.onealfredplace.co.uk @onealfredplace
	The largest provider of serviced office accommodation in the world and still run by original founder, Mark Dixon. A range of packages include Virtual Office, Business Lounge access and serviced offices. Gold Businessworld membership starts at £39 per month. The company has recently launched Regus Connect to test 10 locations that will connect freelancers and interns.	www.regus.co.uk @regus_uk

Impact Hub	*London (Westminster, Kings Cross, Islington)*
The Clubhouse London	*London (Mayfair)*
The Office Group	*14 spaces in London and one in Bristol*
The Old Church School	*Somerset*
The Trampery	*London (Shoreditch, Clerkenwell & London Fields)*
The Workbox	*Penzance*

	With connections to Hubs across the globe, this group of co-working spaces is open to companies with a social mission. Packages range from £125 to £475 per month depending on number of visits.	www.impacthub.net @impacthub
	A business club, lounge and meeting space. Become a Club member for one to two day use per week for £155 per month, or a House member with unlimited access for £225 per month.	www.theclubhouselondon.com @TCHLondon
	Provides flexible offices, meeting rooms and ClubRooms as drop-in workspaces. For this, there is no monthly membership, you simply pay by the hour plus a £25 registration fee.	www.theofficegroup.co.uk @theofficegroup
	Packages start at £20 and rise to £250 per month for unlimited use of the space.	www.theoldchurchschool.co.uk
	Focused on the creative and tech sectors. Full-time desks priced at circa £300 per month and drop-in rates at £25 per day.	www.thetrampery.com @thetrampery
	If you'd like to work by the sea, this is the one for you! Stunning views with a special rate, on application, for start-up businesses and packages then starting at £42 per month to £275 per month for your own lockable office.	www.theworkbox.com @workboxpenzance

Corporate accelerators offer space as part of an accelerator package and were covered on page 198.

"I am very proud to have been the first member of Central Working – they opened up just as I was setting up so it made a lot of sense at the time and it felt great to be part of a new community of members who were all solo business owners like myself. I was also a member of One Alfred Place. Central was more for being part of a community whereas One Alfred Place was a good space for my client meetings where I needed a bit more space and quiet. I have had good clients from both, though this was never the main reason for joining. I have since moved to The Clubhouse which recently opened. It's a private business club but they also run networking events for its members with great speakers and a book club so I suppose it combines the two things I am looking for."

FRANCESCA GEENS, DIGITAL DRAGONFLY

Enterprise Nation @ Somerset House

Seeing the demand from small businesses to get together and learn from experts and peers, Enterprise Nation has opened its own space! Based at Somerset House, the space is a place of education – and HQ for the Enterprise Nation team. Backed by partner brands including Moonfruit, Microsoft, HP, PayPal, Verisign, BT and others, we offer training to thousands of small businesses via practical workshops and meet-ups, manage national projects and campaigns including the Growth Vouchers marketplace, Go & Grow Online and Go Global, and run events on all aspects of starting and growing a business.

There's plenty of activity from which to choose. We look forward to welcoming you!

 **www.enterprisenation.com/events**

Funding

When it comes to funding, ask yourself if you really need it. Results from an Enterprise Nation growth survey showed the majority (54%) of respondents saying they would fund growth from working capital as opposed to taking on debt or loans, or offering equity to investors.

"We have not raised funds to date. We have set up and grown the business using cash flow and a £5,000 Prince's Trust loan. This was through choice and we probably have compromised on growth as a result.

We have been particularly stringent on negotiating and efficient with resources, which I believe has caused us to focus on building a strong business model and foundations. If we had raised money and had surplus cash in the beginning we wouldn't have negotiated as well and I believe this is particularly important with a high volume/low margin industry."

Adam Taylor, Founder, PetShopBowl

If you do decide that funds are what you're after, here's where to look.

Government

Open to any UK business seeking finance of between £1,000 and £1 million, the Enterprise Finance Guarantee (EFG) works through the government providing the lender (likely to be a high street bank) with a guarantee for 75% of each individual loan. The borrower (i.e. you) is responsible for repayment of the full loan and pays a 2% per annum pro-rata premium to the Department for Business Innovation & Skills as a contribution towards the cost of the government guarantee.

Crowdfunding

Without doubt, crowdfunding is on the rise as more small business owners turn to peers and the crowd to raise funds for growth and expansion. There are three main types of crowdfunding:

1. **Reward** – this is where people fund your business in exchange for rewards.
2. **Equity** – this is where the crowd invests in your business in exchange for a percentage of the business.
3. **Loan** – this is where you raise money and repay it with interest.

In raising funds from the crowd, not only do you secure the capital you need but you also attract attention and an audience of potential customers.

Crowdfunding websites

- Crowdfunder: www.crowdfunder.co.uk
- Kickstarter: www.kickstarter.com
- Crowdcube: www.crowdcube.com
- Crowd2Fund: www.crowd2fund.com
- Indiegogo: www.indiegogo.com
- Seedrs: www.seedrs.com

It was crowdfunding with Crowdfunder that gave Snact the capital it needed to increase sales and distribution.

Name: Michael Minch-Dixon

Business: Snact

In asking Snact co-founder, Michael, why the company chose crowdfunding as a route to raise money for their fruit jerky business, he is clear in his reply:

"We saw it as a great way to raise funds, awareness and a following. Some of the other funding opportunities for start-ups such as grants can be quite slow. Crowdfunding gave us the opportunity to do it our way entirely, without restrictions. More importantly, crowdfunding helped us come to the attention of a group of people who support our project and act as a seal of approval for what we're doing. It's also a great way to open up doors through the connections that have been made as a result of the campaign."

It was at Enterprise Nation's Food Exchange event that Michael met crowdfunding platform Crowdfunder and started the conversation as to whether this was the appropriate funding route for Snact expansion.

"Our target was £12,000 and we raised this in less than three weeks! The response was amazing. Securing the funding enabled us to start producing on a scale that's commercially viable and we also needed to change our distribution channels to meet increased output.

The advice we were offered to run our campaign is what I would offer to others: take time to prepare your campaign and think of everything that's involved, particularly the costs of your rewards. Find a way to get people excited about you and your ambitions and get supporters on board before the campaign starts so it looks like there's momentum as soon as the funding page goes live.

Create a sense of urgency (there is some after all if you have a fixed target!) and plan for publicity – articles in newspapers, bloggers, tweets by influential people/organisations. Don't underestimate how much time it'll take and how intense the first weeks will be – you need to be on your computer constantly blasting out news and updates on the campaign. Replying to people takes time, as do the conversations and great connections that come along with crowdfunding. Make it fun and people will get more excited and don't forget to link the value of your rewards to your key demographic."

With funding and a following now in place, Michael and fellow co-founder, Ilana, are taking the business to the next level where it is financially sustainable and selling higher volumes of fruit snacts and tackling more food waste, a key principle on which the company is based.

"I should mention a final benefit of crowdfunding." says Michael "raising funds and credibility through crowdfunding puts us in a stronger position for our next round of funding."

 www.snact.co.uk

 @snactnow

Working capital

Maybe your business needs funds for 'working capital', i.e. an injection of cash to tide you over from one order to the next. If so, consider these options.

Iwoca

Working capital for online retailers, delivering short-term funding with a fast turnaround that enables you to purchase stock and keep the business moving.

> *"With high street bank lending in decline, obtaining finance from traditional sources is often not an option as they have a difficulty in making an accurate assessment of online businesses. Unlike banks, we'll consider alternative data sources, such as a seller's overall feedback scores and online trading history. Within less than 55 seconds of signing up, applicants know how much and at what terms iwoca may lend to them."*
>
> Christoph Rieche, Founder, iwoca
> (**www.iwoca.co.uk**) (**@iwoca**)

Everline

Offering "fast and flexible short-term loans for your business", Everline extends loans of up to 52 weeks to small businesses with a two-year plus trading track record.

"Business applicants simply decide how much they want to borrow, for how many weeks, apply and we calculate the total cost in real-time before they proceed. Once an application is approved, we can deposit the money straight into a business bank account within one business day – and as little as 15 minutes depending on the bank in question."

So far the company has extended loans to franchise owners, online retailers, estate agents, wholesalers, solicitors, high street retailers, hair and beauty salons and business service providers.

 www.everline.com

Funding Circle

If you are a limited company with over two years of filed accounts and a minimum annual turnover of £100,000, borrow between £5,000 and £500,000 with Funding Circle which matches businesses looking for loans with people ready to lend. The online application form takes around 20 minutes to complete and you receive a decision from underwriters within 48 hours.

 www.fundingcircle.com

 @fundingcircle

Angels

Raising investment from angel investors means accessing capital as well as hopefully useful industry contacts who will influence the growth of the business. There are plenty of funds and investors eager to part with their money and back good ideas, and, what's more, the government has made it financially attractive for angels to invest through the Enterprise Investment Scheme, offering up to 30% tax relief to investors, and the Seed

Enterprise Investment Scheme which offers individual income tax relief of 50% and exemption from capital gains tax (CGT) on any proceeds of sale of an SEIS investment.

To be a qualifying company for either EIS or SEIS, visit the HMRC website to ensure you meet the criteria and complete an application. The approval process can take up to three weeks so it's advisable to do this before approaching investors.

EIS Relief: www.hmrc.gov.uk/eis

SEIS Relief: www.hmrc.gov.uk/seedeis

Usually the most ideal route to approach angels is via angel networks. Find details via the UK Business Angels Association.

CEO of the association, Jenny Tooth, outlines the realities of angel investing and how to go about it.

"It's important when you're thinking about the finance needs for your business to consider whether angel investment is right for you. You will have to give up shares in the business in return for the finance and this means losing some of the control you may have had to date. You also need to consider that investors are seeking to make a return (ideally they look for 10x), although angels are patient investors unlike venture capitalists so they are happy to work with you to grow your business over a number of years but you need to be prepared to ultimately exit your business, often by selling to another larger company, to enable the investors and you to realise the value of the shares. So if you feel that you just want to grow your business slowly and not share it with investors, angel investing is not for you.

If you do decide angel investing is the way forward, begin by appreciating the questions investors will have about growth and returns and reflect this in how you present your business proposal.

Show the investor you have an idea which can attract a good share of the market and customers (you don't need to have them yet, but show you know who they are). Show how you will make money from your service or product and that your business model can generate strong revenues over time. Show an understanding of your competitors and why your product/service is better (cheaper, faster, etc.) and how you might maintain this position – and how the business can be scaled over about a five-year period.

Outline why you need the investment, what you will spend it on to make a difference, and finally what else you want from the investors, such as finance or market expertise or strategic advice etc, since angels like to see how they can help.

When presenting your proposal, don't send out a complex business plan; start with a PowerPoint presentation of about 12 slides covering these aspects and have a 2–5 minute pitch ready in case they contact you.

In terms of how to approach angel investors, whilst they can be quite elusive, many of them belong to networks and syndicate groups and so a good way to find them initially is to send your proposal through to the gatekeeper or co-ordinator who will look at your proposal, and if they think it's suitable for their network or group of angels will then get in touch and invite you to meet with them, most likely through a pitch presentation. Many of the angel networks are listed on the UK Business Angels Association website: **www.ukbusinessangelsassociation.org.uk/member/directory**

You can also go to pitching events held in your area, but you may have to pitch at many such events before identifying the investors that are right for your business. However, these can also be good ways to gain experience at pitching.

Finally, if you do find investors interested in your business, make sure you do your due diligence on them to ensure that they have the finance and experience you need to grow your business. You could be involved with them for some time so it's important to feel you have the right people on board."

 www.ukbusinessangelsassociation.org.uk

 @UKBAngels

Banks

The banks are worth approaching with a business plan and good trading record as overdraft or loan facilities could be on offer.

The Business Banking Association has created a useful website, Better Business Finance (**www.betterbusinessfinance.co.uk/finance**), which brings into one place a range of finance providers including angels, regional funds, government schemes and banks. Simply search on your geographic location, industry, and the amount of finance required.

Jim Riley and twin brother, Geoff, each invested £1,000 in their business at the outset and haven't had to raise funds since. Their business is now turning over millions and they have just invested £100,000 in a start-up elearning business. Together they have taken practically every step in this book. They have outsourced, productised, gone global, secured support, and gone full circle to become angels.

Name: Jim Riley

Business: Tutor2u

"The idea for Tutor2u came from Geoff's teaching (he is a well-known economics teacher) and my experience in corporate strategy and finance. We just wanted a project we could work on together. We started with a simple website and packed it full of free content for teachers, based around the mantra – 'If we build it, they will come' (hat-tip to *Field of Dreams*!)."

The traffic did come and the site now attracts over 30 million unique users per year. The brothers have adopted a freemium model meaning most of the content is free to users with an option to upgrade (and pay) for premium value-added products and services.

"We have a team of around 75–100 teachers and subject experts who write the materials (e.g. blogs, revision guides, teaching activities), predominantly based in the UK but increasingly from international schools too."

The business generates money from selling online products such as digital textbooks, revision guides and lesson activities, online advertising and now from events too, with a growing programme of professional training courses for teachers and revision workshops for students.

This income, and traffic, comes from across the globe with the company exporting to schools and colleges in over 80 countries.

"In 2013, for the first time we took our CPD programme directly to our international customers, running a two-day series in Dubai. It was very popular, so we're now extending to Mumbai and Singapore."

The company promotes itself through direct mailings to UK schools, email marketing (with over 20,000 teachers registered to receive newsletters), RSS feed syndication, Twitter, a Facebook page with 40k+ fans, and organic SEO on account of publishing lots of relevant and high quality content.

"Our face-to-face events are also a very effective method of promotion. We get thousands of our customers paying to spend time with us – a great way to conduct market research and let them know what else is going on!"

To minimise costs and maximise input from specialists, the company has outsourced telephone handling to manage overflow call handling, graphic design, website coding, printing and warehousing.

To achieve its plans, Jim signed up to be part of the government's Growth Accelerator programme with an ambition to double turnover.

"We left the home office and moved to a shared service office in the village about six years ago. It's a small office with four of us in it but together we're serving 30 million+ website visitors!"

 **www.tutor2u.net**

 **@tutor2u**

Conclusion

I hope these pages have provided you with the information and inspiration you need to get going and growing.

There's never been a better time to grow your business whilst staying nimble and keeping costs under control.

Build a multinational, multi-thousand/million pound business from home? You bet it's possible!

Best wishes with your efforts and I hope you'll decide to join Enterprise Nation so we can support you along the way.

Emma Jones

Enterprise Nation

With Thanks

With thanks to the experts and commentators featured:

Anna Rigby	*John Lewis*
Andy Law	*Entrepreneur and mentor*
Catherine Hayes	*HSBC*
Chris Book	*Bardowl*
David Speakman	*Travel Counsellors*
Ed Faulkner	*Virgin Books*
Emily Coltman	*FreeAgent*
Gordon Tempest-Hay	*Blue Rubicon*
Graeme Payne	*Bird & Bird LLP*
James Gilmour	*Simply Business*
Joanna Penn	*The Creative Penn*
Joanna Tall	*Offtoseemylawyer.com*
Jenny Tooth	*UK Business Angels Association*
John Hayes	*iContact*
Matt McNeil	*SignUp To*
Paul Monaghan	*The Franchising Centre*
Paul Stafford	*British Franchise Association*
Matt Truman	*Truestart Capital*
Rekha Mehr	*Pistachio Rose*
Dr Stuart Brodie	*Direct-selling expert*
Suzanne Dibble	*Suzanne Dibble*
Tamsin Fox-Davies	*Constant Contact*

Join Enterprise Nation and Grow Your Business on a Budget!

Enterprise Nation is the UK's most active small business network. As well as writing books like this, we also provide businesses like yours with a daily blog, lively events, and campaigning voice to government.

Join Enterprise Nation for just £30 a year and benefit from:

- consultation calls with advisers
- free eBooks & webinars
- member meet-ups
- invitations to member-only events
- 25% off all Enterprise Nation products and services
- exclusive offers on business essentials
- access to member forum to ask questions and share ideas
- an Enterprise Nation member badge

Plus more!

Simply visit www.enterprisenation.com/join and join today.